THE POCKET HOLE DRILLING JIG PROJECT BOOK

DANNY PROULX

POPULAR WOODWORKING BOOKS

CINCINNATI, OHIO
www.popularwoodworking.com

read this important safety notice

To prevent accidents, keep safety in mind while you work. Use the safety guards installed on power equipment; they are for your protection. When working on power equipment, keep fingers away from saw blades, wear safety goggles to prevent injuries from flying wood chips and sawdust, wear headphones to protect your hearing, and consider installing a dust vacuum to reduce the amount of airborne sawdust in your woodshop. Don't wear loose clothing, such as neckties or shirts with loose sleeves, or jewelry, such as rings, necklaces or bracelets, when working on power equipment. Tie back long hair to prevent it from getting caught in your equipment. People who are sensitive to certain chemicals should check the chemical content of any product before using it. The authors and editors who compiled this book have tried to make the contents as accurate and correct as possible. Plans, illustrations, photographs and text have been carefully checked. All instructions, plans and projects should be carefully read, studied and understood before beginning construction. In some photos, power tool guards have been removed to more clearly show the operation being demonstrated. Always use all safety guards and attachments that come with your power tools. Due to the variability of local conditions, construction materials, skill levels, etc., neither the author nor Popular Woodworking Books assumes any responsibility for any accidents, injuries, damages or other losses incurred resulting from the material presented in this book. Prices listed for supplies and equipment were current at the time of publication and are subject to change. Glass shelving should have all edges polished and must be tempered. Untempered glass shelves may shatter and can cause serious bodily injury. Tempered shelves are very strong and if they break will just crumble, minimizing personal injury.

metric conversion chart

TO CONVERT	TO	MULTIPLY BY
Inches	Centimeters	2.54
Centimeters	Inches	0.4
Feet	Centimeters	30.5
Centimeters	Feet	0.03
Yards	Meters	0.9
Meters	Yards	1.1
Sq. Inches	Sq. Centimeters	6.45
Sq. Centimeters	Sq. Inches	0.16
Sq. Feet	Sq. Meters	0.09
Sq. Meters	Sq. Feet	10.8
Sq. Yards	Sq. Meters	0.8
Sq. Meters	Sq. Yards	1.2
Pounds	Kilograms	0.45
Kilograms	Pounds	2.2
Ounces	Grams	28.4
Grams	Ounces	0.035

Visit our Web site at www.popularwoodworking.com for information on more resources for woodworkers.

Other fine Popular Woodworking Books are available from your local bookstore or direct from the publisher.

15   14   13   12   9   8   7   6

Library of Congress Cataloging-in-Publication Data

Proulx, Danny.
    The pocket hole drilling jig project book / by Danny Proulx
        p. cm.
    Includes index.
        ISBN 1-55870-687-9 (alk. paper)
    1. Woodwork--Amateurs' manuals.   2. Joinery-Amateurs' manuals.   3. Jigs and fixtures--Amateurs' manuals. 4. Furniture making--Amateurs' manuals. I. Title.
TT185.P77   2004   2003044221
684'.08--dc22

ACQUISITIONS EDITOR: Jim Stack
EDITED BY: Jennifer Ziegler
DESIGNED BY: Brian Roeth
LAYOUT ARTIST: Christine Long
PRODUCTION COORDINATED BY: Mark Griffin
STEP PHOTOGRAPHY BY: Danny Proulx
LEAD PHOTOGRAPHER: Michael Bowie
COMPUTER ILLUSTRATIONS BY: Len Churchill
WORKSHOP SITE: Rideau Cabinets

about THE author

Danny Proulx is the owner of Rideau Cabinets and is a contributing editor for *CabinetMaker* magazine. He also contributes freelance articles for *Canadian Woodworking, Canadian Home Workshop, Popular Woodworking* and other magazines.

His earlier books include *Build Your Own Kitchen Cabinets, The Kitchen Cabinetmaker's Building and Business Manual, How to Build Classic Garden Furniture, Smart Shelving & Storage Solutions, Fast & Easy Techniques for Building Modern Cabinetry, Building More Classic Garden Furniture, Building Cabinet Doors & Drawers, Build Your Own Home Office Furniture, Display Cases You Can Build, Building Frameless Kitchen Cabinets* and *Building Woodshop Workstations.*

You can reach Danny via his Web site, www.cabinetmaking.com, and he can be reached by e-mail at danny@cabinetmaking.com.

acknowledgements

Once again my team has been the major reason for any success this book will enjoy. My wife, Gale, is constantly helpful and supportive, as is my father-in-law and assistant, Jack Chaters. Special thanks to Cody, who built the clock in project eleven.

Michael Bowie of Lux Photography continues to show his amazing photographic talents and is responsible for the cover and chapter lead shots. He advises and guides me as I shoot the step-by-step photos for each project. His concern to produce the best results and his expert advice contribute greatly to the final product.

Len Churchill of Lenmark Communications is the talented illustrator who has been working with me and producing the amazing project drawings. He is one of the best illustrators in the business and has an impressive understanding of the woodworking projects he's asked to draw.

As always, the Popular Woodworking Books staff continues to be unbelievably supportive. It's a team with great depth and knowledge. Thanks to editor Jim Stack, Jenny Ziegler, Brian Roeth, Jennifer Johnson and so many others who are a part of every page in this book.

technical support

The following companies have been a tremendous help in creating this book.

Kreg Tool Company
Jimmy Jigs
Trend Machinery & Cutting Tools Ltd.
McFeely's Square Drive Screws

I often turn to a number of companies for advice and supplies. They are always helpful and are a source of valuable information. They are major players in the creation of my books, and I've listed them in the back of this book under the heading "Suppliers." I'd appreciate your support of these fine companies.

TABLE OF contents

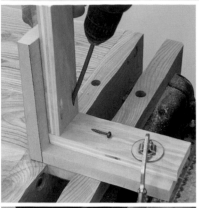

introduction . . . 6

CHAPTER ONE
equipment and accessories . . . 8

CHAPTER TWO
pocket hole joinery applications . . . 16

PROJECT ONE
face-frame and case joinery . . . 24

PROJECT TWO
tall bookcase . . . 34

PROJECT THREE
quilt rack . . . 42

PROJECT FOUR
window bench . . . 48

PROJECT FIVE
chest of drawers . . . 56

PROJECT SIX
kitchen display and storage cabinet . . . 68

PROJECT SEVEN
coffee and end tables . . . 82

PROJECT EIGHT
sofa or hall table . . . 90

PROJECT NINE
framed mirror . . . 98

PROJECT TEN
pendulum wall clock . . . 106

PROJECT ELEVEN
child's wall clock . . . 118

suppliers . . . 124

index . . . 126

introduction

**This is a wood joinery book with one specific purpose —
to explore the many uses of pocket hole joinery.**

I'm sure that some purists will frown upon the use of this joinery method. However, it allows a woodworker to complete projects without the use of expensive machinery. This important joinery system is well worth studying. Pocket hole joinery is simply one more step in the ongoing search for woodworking knowledge.

Professional and advanced woodworkers can also make use of pocket hole joinery because it is a viable option for certain applications. Face-frame construction for cabinetwork is a perfect example of one of these applications. Many cabinetmakers use this joinery method on a daily basis in their shops.

Pocket hole joinery enables woodworkers who don't have a large shop with a lot of tools to build projects they couldn't normally complete. The satisfaction of building something creates interest in our hobby and promotes its growth. A hobby that continues to grow benefits everyone.

One of my greatest joys in woodworking is to explore new equipment and methods. Modern building materials, newly developed tools and methods of joinery, as well as the latest hardware systems, make this hobby interesting and vibrant. I think we would all get bored very quickly if there was only one way to build a project. Thankfully, there are dozens of ways to join wood, and using pocket holes is just one other option.

Pocket hole joinery doesn't always have to be hidden. Wood filler plugs, designed specifically for pocket holes, are available in four or five wood species. You don't have to use the same wood type for the filler plugs, either! A couple of projects in this book will have exposed holes with contrasting wood plugs as a design feature.

I'll provide details about many of the pocket hole jigs that are available. You'll learn about those in chapter one, and I'll show you how to build your own jig as an option to the commercial versions. I'll also detail the screw options and their use, because there are different views and opinions as to the style of fasteners that should be used.

In chapter two I'll show and explain some of the joinery that can be accomplished using pocket holes. The applications are limitless with this joinery system, and new uses are being developed each month. I've seen some creative and intelligent joinery procedures using pocket holes, and I'm sure there are hundreds more yet to be developed.

The remainder of the chapters feature projects that can be built using pocket hole joinery. I have tried to restrict the number of power tools needed for each project so those of you with limited equipment can build your own version. Woodworkers who are fortunate enough to have a shop with lots of equipment can modify some of the designs to suit their needs. I detail one joinery method in each chapter and offer a few options that you can explore.

Pocket hole joinery is a relatively new method and, like biscuit joinery, will most likely take some time to be widely accepted. However, the practice of boring holes at an angle and using wood dowels to secure the joint is an old and accepted method. That system has been refined because we now have modern hardware that takes the place of wood dowels. The screws offer a distinct advantage over dowels because the parts are drawn together and clamping isn't a requirement.

For those of you who think pocket hole joinery isn't as strong as traditional wood joints, look at a test report on the Kreg Tool Company's Web site, at www.kregtool.com/testreport.pdf. This joinery system is gaining in popularity every day, making believers out of woodworkers who try the system. Experiment with the techniques yourself and you'll soon realize that pocket hole joinery should be another of your considered options when joining materials.

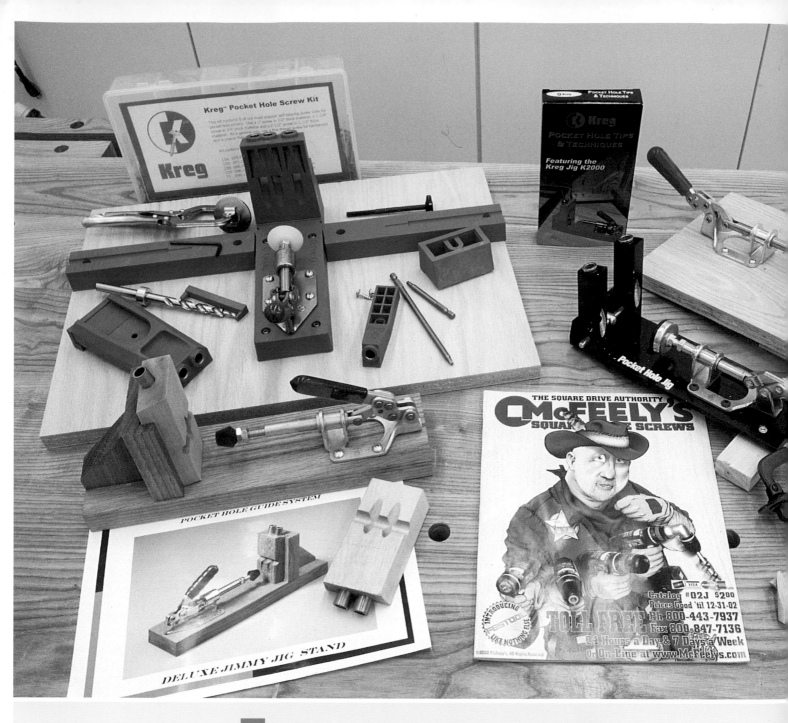

equipment
AND accessories

A NUMBER OF COMPANIES MANUFAC-ture pocket hole jigs, and a few specialize in making and supplying different styles of fastening screws. All the machines accomplish the same task of drilling a counterbored hole, at an angle, to permit the use of a screw fastener to join wood parts. I want to explore the differences, however, in jig construction, clamping devices and the jig's use in a vertical or horizontal position.

I will also show how to build your own custom jig. I don't believe the shop-made jig is a lot less expensive than the commercial models, but it can be configured to suit your applications. If you build face frames on a continuous basis, for example, you may want a custom pocket hole jig fixed in a certain location.

Providing price list information wouldn't serve a useful purpose because equipment costs are always changing. Also, sales, end-of-line bargains and promotional offers may be available when you decide to buy your jig, so information on the current price wouldn't apply. I suggest you look at all the jigs, check out the construction and machining, the ease of operation for your application, as well as the warranty and dealer support, before buying equipment.

Sometimes cost alone isn't the only factor!

The Kreg Tool Company's Web site has a great answer to the question, "What is pocket hole joinery?"

"Pocket hole joinery in its simplest terms is drilling a hole at an angle into one workpiece and then joining it to a second workpiece with a self-tapping screw. This technique was actually invented by the Egyptians as they clamped two workpieces together and then bored a hole at an angle from the outside workpiece into the second workpiece. They then inserted a dowel with some glue and cut it off flush with the surface. This technique continued to evolve over the years into two main joinery methods, doweling and more recently pocket hole joinery. The modern pocket hole joint grew in popularity with the creation of the self-tapping screw in the 1980s, which eliminated the need to drill into the second workpiece altogether."

In this chapter I'll look at four pocket hole jigs: the Kreg Jig K2000, the Trend Pocket Hole Jig, a pocket hole guide system from Jimmy Jigs, and a shop-built jig. I'll also detail pocket hole screws from Kreg and McFeely's, as well as drill bit styles.

KREG TOOL COMPANY'S K2000 POCKET HOLE JIG IS SHOWN AT LEFT.

The K2000 is one of several pocket hole jigs manufactured by the Kreg Tool Company. This jig comes with a complete kit with support wings, spacers for drilling stock up to 1½" thick, a Mini Jig, drill-stop collar and sample screw pack.

The Kreg jig is made of glass-reinforced plastic with three drill guides and a toggle clamp. The wings help support wide stock and have a built-in template for setting the drill-stop collar. Drill depth is determined by the locking collar position and must be adjusted for different stock thicknesses. The K2000 ProPack system is contained in a plastic case.

This Kreg jig uses a three-hole configuration and is handy for drilling stock of varying widths without having to move a board. Like many other quality jigs, the Kreg jig has drill guides made of hardened steel. This company manufactures one of the largest lines of pocket hole jigs, so you should be able to find one to suit your budget and requirements.

THIS POCKET HOLE JIG IS FROM TREND MACHINERY & CUTTING TOOLS LTD.

Trend Machinery & Cutting Tools Ltd. is based in England and manufactures all types of cutting tools, power tools, woodworking jigs and a pocket hole jig. The Trend jig can also be purchased as a complete kit with face clamp, drill bit and collar, two square drive bits and 100 pan head screws.

The jig was introduced in 2002 and features hardened bushings and an all-metal construction. The adjustable drill guides can be locked in various positions to accommodate different widths of stock. The easy-to-read scale allows the guide columns to be equally positioned. Stock can be drilled up to a maximum of 1½".

THIS IS THE PORTER-CABLE COMMERCIAL POCKET HOLE CUTTER.

This isn't a book about commercial pocket hole cutters, but it's interesting to note that professional cabinet shops use the pocket system as one of their standard joints. Companies like Porter-Cable and Kreg Tools manufacture single- and double-router cutting systems for high-volume shops. These motorized, high-speed units can cut hundreds of pocket holes in a very short time.

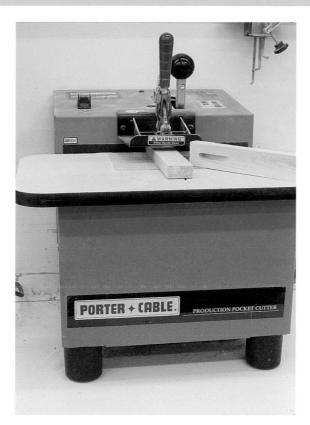

THE PHOTO ABOVE SHOWS POCKET HOLE SCREWS.

There are as many pocket hole screw types as there are pocket hole jigs. Screws are the main ingredients in achieving a solid pocket hole joint, so you must have the right screw to get perfect results. There are screws for hardwoods and softwoods, as well as different thicknesses of material. The goal is to use the proper length of screw in a correctly positioned hole. Ideally, the screw should cross both pieces to be joined at their center line, or half the thickness of each workpiece. Screw threads should be clear of the workpiece that has the drilled pocket hole, as the screw bottoms or tightens in the hole. The nonthreaded shaft can only spin in that situation and thus draws both pieces tightly together. If the threads are tracking in both pieces of wood, the joint will bridge as the screw head bottoms, leaving a gap between boards.

The photograph above illustrates a few of the pocket hole screws that are available. From left to right, first is a 1¼" long No. 6 square drive, coarse-threaded softwood screw; a fine-threaded hardwood version; a No. 8 square drive type with a larger head; a trademarked PocketMax No. 8 square drive screw that's 2⅝" long; and a Pocket-Max No. 8 square drive screw (2⅝" long) with a corrosion-resistant coating for outdoor building projects like fences and garden furniture.

THIS IS JIMMY JIGS' POCKET HOLE GUIDE SYSTEM.

The Jimmy Jig is made in Ontario, Canada. This simple jig is well made and comes with a lifetime guarantee.

Jimmy Jigs' pocket hole jig is made of wood, coated with a resin stain. It has heat-hardened bushings that guide the drill bit into the board. Their system consists of two portable units and three tabletop units. The single and double guide blocks can be interchanged in the stand or used as a portable drill guide that's clamped on the board to be drilled.

Building a Shop-Made Pocket Hole Jig

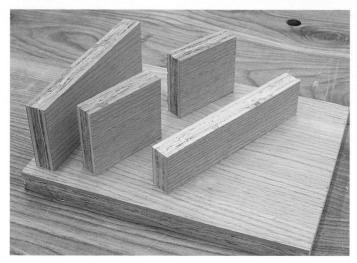

1 Cut five pieces of ¾"-thick plywood for the jig. You'll need a baseboard that's 8" wide by 10" long, a backboard 2½" high by 6¾" long, two supports that are 2½" high by 3" long, and a bottom cleat 1½" wide by 6¾" long.

2 Attach the backboard to the baseboard, flush with one 8"-wide end, using glue and 1½" wood screws from the underside of the baseboard. Center the backboard on the baseboard.

3 Secure one of the supports to the backboard, using screws and glue. The support is aligned flush with one end of the backboard. I used two 1¼" wood screws through the backboard and one from the underside to anchor this support.

4 The single pocket hole guide I purchased has a hole through the side. Drive a 2"-long wood screw through that hole into the support's side edge to secure the drill guide. These pocket hole drill guides are available at most woodworking supply stores.

5 Attach the remaining support block to the backboard, using only three wood screws. Do not use any adhesives on this support block in case the drill guide needs to be replaced. Two screws through the backboard and one through the baseboard will secure the support block.

6 The bottom cleat is installed on the underside of the base-board with 1¼"-long wood screws and glue. It will be used to hold the jig securely in my bench vise when drilling pocket holes.

7 Install a horizontal toggle clamp, being sure to locate it so the travel is correct. You should be able to clamp boards ranging in thickness from ⅝" to 1½" by adjusting the threaded shaft.

8 To complete your jig, you may want to drill holes to store the step drill and collar, as well as the extra drill-guide bushing.

I purchased a pocket hole drill bit at a woodworking store and noticed it had a cone-shaped end. Both Kreg and Trend supplied a square-ended bit, similar to a brad-point-style bit, with their kits.

I tested both drill bit styles and prefer the square-ended brad-type bit because of the flat-bottomed hole it produces. The pocket screws, many of them having a flat head, appear to seat better in the hole.

THIS IS A DRILL BIT STOP COLLAR SETTING.

To prevent drilling into your jig base, slip the drill bit into the guide. Loosen the collar and rest the bit point on a coin. Move the stop collar to the top of the drill-guide bushing and tighten the locking screw. That setting will be correct for most pocket hole drilling.

In some cases, you may need extra depth to completely hide the pocket hole screw beneath the workpiece surface. Simply raise the collar slightly to deepen the hole. For example, if you plan on using pocket hole filler plugs, and the screw has a large round head, the hole must be a little deeper to achieve a proper fit for the wood plug. I'll be using wood plugs as a decorative element in some of the projects to illustrate this situation.

pocket hole
joinery applications

POCKET HOLE JOINERY YIELDS A versatile joint that can be used in many situations. In fact, it's extremely useful in specialized areas, such as angle joinery, where conventional techniques are difficult and complicated.

In this chapter I'll detail some of the many joinery options you can use in your shop. These techniques will be applied in the following project chapters to illustrate their value. But remember, like any other woodworking joint, a pocket hole joint is only as good as the techniques and hardware used to create the joint. You must have the correct screw, well-machined surfaces for the adhesives and the proper pocket hole depth.

One of the major issues with pocket hole joinery is the length and type of screw used. Screw length is based on the material thickness to be joined. Fine-threaded screws are generally used in hardwoods, and coarse threads are for softwoods and particleboards. Typically, screws are available in 1" and $1\frac{1}{4}$" lengths, as well as special lengths for applications that require an extralong screw. However, for the majority of your joinery applications, you will be using a $1\frac{1}{4}$" fine- or coarse-threaded screw.

Proper screw length is critical. A screw that's too long can do a great deal of damage to a finished surface. If the screw is too short, the joint may fail. Never assume the screw length is correct, particularly for angle joints. Test the screw on scrap lumber to assure yourself that your joint application versus screw length is correct. It's well worth the extra time and effort.

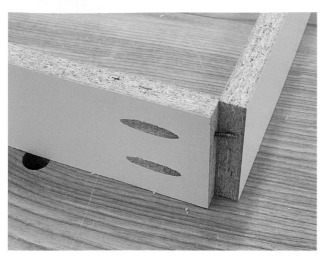

TESTING THE JOINT

Always test a new joint with scrap lumber before assembling finished boards. Drill a pocket hole and drive the screw into the hole until it bottoms. Hold the receiving board in place and check the screw depth for proper placement.

CLAMPING THE JOINT

Use a wide-faced clamp, like the one shown, to hold and align both pieces of the joint when driving pocket hole screws. The boards can also be clamped to a flat surface with woodworking clamps as long as the pieces are properly aligned.

SOFTWOOD JOINERY

I sometimes find that the standard $1\frac{1}{4}$"-long coarse-threaded screws for softwoods don't always grip the workpieces properly. The screws will strip their threaded hole, which could lead to a joint failure.

If the softwood boards you're joining are 2" or wider, try a $1\frac{1}{2}$"-long coarse-threaded pocket hole screw. It has been a much better fastener for softwoods with my projects. Try a few tests with different woods and screws to determine your preferences.

CORNER-JOINT ASSEMBLY JIG

Build a right-angle support jig for your shop. Use any material to build this jig, but make sure the joint is square. Attach a strip on the underside so it can be clamped in a vise. The jig makes pocket hole corner-joint assembly simple, accurate and fast.

T-JOINTS

The T-joint is one of the most common pocket hole applications. It's often used to assemble face frames in the kitchen cabinetmaking industry. The joint offers many benefits to a woodworker because it's hidden, strong and quick to assemble.

L-JOINTS

The L-joint is another commonly used joinery application. It's the same assembly procedure as the T-joint on a face frame, but is used at the corner of the frame.

EDGE JOINERY

If you have an application where a number of narrower boards must be joined to form a panel, pocket hole edge joinery is a good application. The boards can be joined edge to edge with glue and held firmly with pocket hole screws until the adhesive sets. You don't need any clamps for this application.

CORNER MITER JOINTS

You can easily use pocket hole joinery for 45° mitered joints. Cut the angles, then drill pocket holes in the workpiece with the cut edge on the jig platform. As long as you take care to align the hole properly, this can be an effective corner joint.

CORNER MITER JOINTS

This corner joint works best when the material being joined is 2" or wider. Thinner boards can be joined, but the alignment is critical, so I limit the use of this joint to wide stock.

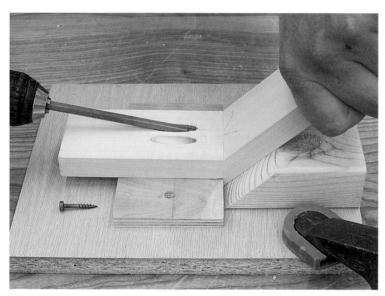

FACE-ANGLE JOINERY

Two boards can be joined at any angle by building the jig shown in the photograph. The joint isn't created by cutting each board at half the final angle (a 45° joint normally has each board cut at 22½°), but by leaving one square and cutting the full angle on the other. The backrest on the jig, as illustrated in the photograph, is cut to the final joint angle.

For example, if I wanted two boards at 45° to each other, the jig's backrest needs to be cut at that angle. The board with the angle cut is placed on the backrest, and the square-cut board, with pocket holes drilled, is screwed to the angled board. You'll also need to install a spacer under the square-cut board so the inside face edges of both boards are aligned before joining.

FACE-ANGLE JOINERY

This method results in a joint with an overhang on the front face. That overhang can be removed with a plane or sander. The result is two boards, joined at the required angle, with an offset joint line. It's a great joinery application that's easy to do and unique to pocket holes.

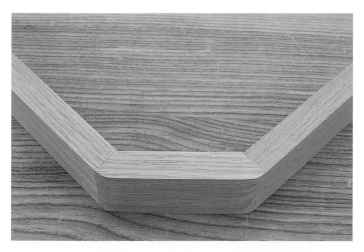

FACE-ANGLE JOINERY

Face-angle joinery has dozens of applications. Once the joint is secure, the face edge can be sanded round to create some interesting visual effects. Any angle can be used and any amount of forming (sanding) can be done to the wood. This application could be used as a light guard, a curved front on a cabinet or in dozens of other furniture designs.

OFFSET JOINERY

Boards joined using pocket hole joinery don't always have to align at their edges or ends. You can create an offset — often a design requirement when building tables and chairs.

OFFSET JOINERY

The offset is accomplished by cutting a rabbet in a spacer block. Rabbet depth will be equal to the amount of offset you need. Clamp the spacer on the board without the pocket holes, and butt the leg against the spacer jig. Drive screws into the joint and remove the clamp. The result is an identical offset on all legs.

LEG AND RAIL JOINERY

Pocket holes are drilled in the rails, and screws secure the assembly to the tabletop. On sheet material tops like particleboard or plywood, expansion and contraction isn't an issue, so the screws can be driven in standard pocket holes.

However, if you are using a solid-wood top (either one piece or a glue-up of smaller boards), wood movement must be taken into account. In this circumstance, I drill standard pocket holes in the rail, then use a drill bit that is two times larger in diameter than the point on the pocket hole step drill bit, to slightly enlarge the holes. This technique will allow the solid-wood top to move if necessary, without splitting.

LEG AND RAIL JOINERY

Driving screws, when working with leg and rail joints, can be crowded at times. If that's the case, use a small socket wrench and drive bit in the appropriate socket to install the pocket screws.

DRAWER-BOX CONSTRUCTION

Coarse-threaded pocket hole screws work well when joining particleboard. In fact, the coarse thread on pocket hole screws is almost the same pattern as a particleboard screw.

I often use $1\frac{1}{4}$"-long screws to join drawer boxes made with $\frac{5}{8}$"-thick melamine particleboard. A drawer face hides the front, and the back panel with the pocket holes is hidden when the drawer is in the cabinet.

COUNTERTOP BACKBOARDS

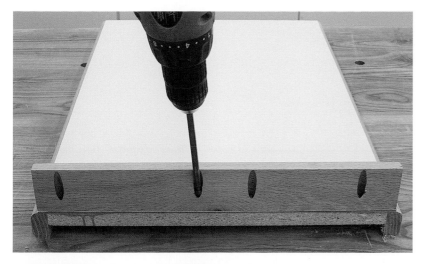

Backboards, sometimes called splashboards, can be securely fastened to any countertop using pocket hole joinery. The back face of the board faces the wall, so the holes are hidden.

INSTALLING WOOD EDGES

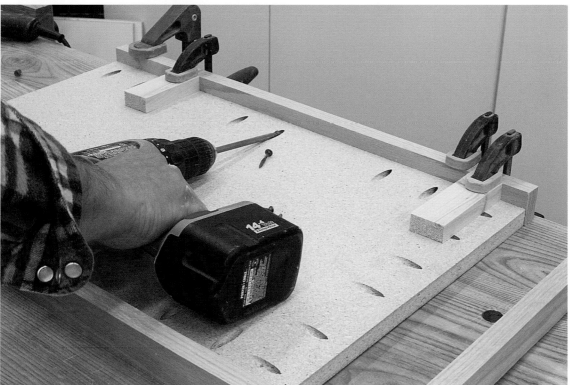

You can use pocket holes and glue to easily install solid-wood edging to any sheet material. Be certain that edging and sheet stock are securely clamped so the top face will be perfectly aligned and flush.

Inexpensive table-tops can be made using this method. This application is often used to replace solid-wood tops.

EXPOSED POCKET HOLES

Wood plugs are available, so pocket holes don't always have to be hidden. I will be using this technique in the project section of this book to create attractive joinery design elements.

Maple, oak and walnut plugs are readily available, so the visual effect of your finished project can be increased by using contrasting-colored plugs. A piece of furniture built from maple, with exposed walnut plugs, is dramatic.

face-frame AND case joinery

THE PROJECT IN THIS CHAPTER ISN'T about a specific-size cabinet. It's primarily about the theory and assembly techniques used for face-frame and case joinery with pocket holes. You can build the cabinet shown using the given dimensions, but illustrating the techniques used to construct any size cabinet, with a face frame, is the goal.

The term *case joinery* is commonly used to describe a cabinet built with sheet material. Display, kitchen, bathroom and commercial cabinets all fall under this description. The *case* is the box or cabinet carcass, and with this style a solid-wood face frame is applied. Frameless-style case joinery uses the same techniques and carcass style, but instead of a solid-wood frame, veneer edge tape is applied.

There are a few different application styles for face-frame cabinets. In some instances, such as kitchen and bathroom cabinets, the inside edge of the face frame is flush with the inside surface of the cabinet side, and the frame stiles (vertical members) overhang the cabinet's outside dimension. The style used in this project, where the outside edges of the face frame are flush with the outside face of the cabinet sides, is more of a furniture style.

Using the face-frame system that's described in this chapter means a special type of hidden-hinge mounting plate will be used, and cleats must be added to the cabinet sides to install bottom- or side-mounted drawer glides. However, it's a popular cabinet style and the hinge/drawer glide changes are not a major issue. Typical applications of this cabinet style include entertainment units, bedside tables, storage cabinets and pantry or sofa end table cabinets, to name a few.

I haven't drilled holes for an adjustable shelf, but it's one option you may want. If so, be sure to drill the holes before you begin step 1. Study the techniques as you progress through the building process and you'll quickly realize that this cabinet style can be used in many different applications.

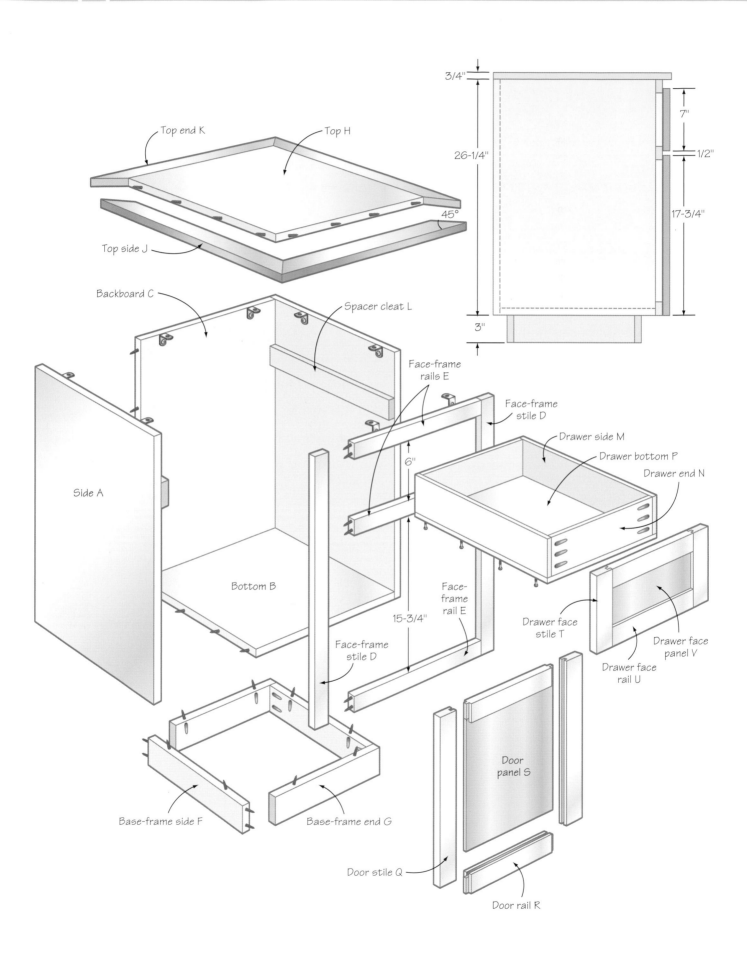

Top end K

Top H

Top side J

45°

3/4"

26-1/4"

7"

1/2"

17-3/4"

3"

Backboard C

Spacer cleat L

Face-frame rails E

Face-frame stile D

Drawer side M

Drawer bottom P

Drawer end N

Side A

6"

Bottom B

Face-frame rail E

Drawer face stile T

15-3/4"

Face-frame stile D

Drawer face panel V

Drawer face rail U

Base-frame side F

Base-frame end G

Door panel S

Door stile Q

Door rail R

inches (millimeters)

REFERENCE	QUANTITY	PART	STOCK	THICKNESS	(mm)	WIDTH	(mm)	LENGTH	(mm)	COMMENTS
A	2	sides	veneer PB	$^{11}/_{16}$	(18)	18	(457)	$26^1/_4$	(666)	
B	1	bottom	veneer PB	$^{11}/_{16}$	(18)	$14^5/_8$	(372)	18	(457)	
C	1	backboard	veneer PB	$^{11}/_{16}$	(18)	$14^5/_8$	(372)	$25^9/_{16}$	(649)	
D	2	face-frame stiles	solid wood	$^3/_4$	(19)	$1^1/_2$	(38)	$26^1/_4$	(666)	
E	3	face-frame rails	solid wood	$^3/_4$	(19)	$1^1/_2$	(38)	13	(330)	
F	2	base-frame sides	veneer PB	$^{11}/_{16}$	(18)	3	(76)	$13^3/_8$	(340)	
G	2	base-frame ends	veneer PB	$^{11}/_{16}$	(18)	3	(76)	12	(305)	
H	1	top	veneer ply	$^3/_4$	(19)	15	(381)	$16^3/_4$	(425)	
J	2	top sides	solid wood	$^3/_4$	(19)	$1^1/_2$	(38)	$19^3/_4$	(502)	mitered
K	2	top ends	solid wood	$^3/_4$	(19)	$1^1/_2$	(38)	18	(457)	mitered
L	2	spacer cleats	solid wood	$^{13}/_{16}$	(21)	$1^1/_2$	(38)	$17^1/_4$	(438)	
M	2	drawer sides	veneer PB	$^{11}/_{16}$	(18)	$4^5/_{16}$	(110)	$17^3/_4$	(451)	
N	2	drawer ends	veneer PB	$^{11}/_{16}$	(18)	$4^5/_{16}$	(110)	$10^5/_8$	(270)	
P	1	drawer bottom	veneer PB	$^{11}/_{16}$	(18)	12	(305)	$17^3/_4$	(451)	
Q	2	door stiles	hardwood	$^3/_4$	(19)	$2^1/_4$	(57)	$17^3/_4$	(451)	
R	2	door rails	hardwood	$^3/_4$	(19)	$2^1/_4$	(57)	11	(279)	
S	1	door panel	veneer ply	$^1/_4$	(6)	$10^7/_8$	(276)	$14^5/_8$	(372)	
T	2	drawer face stiles	hardwood	$^3/_4$	(19)	$2^1/_4$	(57)	7	(178)	
U	2	drawer face rails	hardwood	$^3/_4$	(19)	$1^1/_2$	(38)	11	(279)	
V	1	drawer face panel	veneer ply	$^1/_4$	(6)	$10^7/_8$	(276)	$5^3/_8$	(137)	

Note: PB = particleboard.

hardware AND supplies

Pocket hole screws: $1^1/_4$" (32mm)

Wood screws: $^5/_8$" (16mm), $1^1/_4$" (32mm)

PB screws: 2" (51mm)

Finishing nails: 2" (51mm)

Glue

Wood putty

Wood veneer tape

Right-angle metal brackets

Drawer glides

Hinges and hinge plates

Knobs/handles

1 Drill three pocket holes at each end on the underside of the bottom B. Use glue and $1\frac{1}{4}$"-long pocket hole screws to join the bottom board to the sides A. The bottom board is aligned flush with the lower ends of the side boards.

2 Cut the backboard C and drill three pocket holes on each side and three on the bottom edge. The backboard is inset and flush with the back edges of the sides A. Again, use glue and $1\frac{1}{4}$"-long pocket hole screws to secure the backboard.

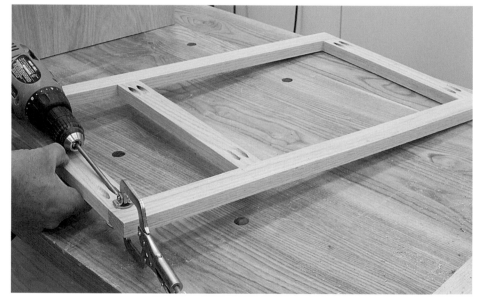

3 The face frame is constructed with two stiles D (vertical members) and three rails E (horizontal members). There are three rails because this cabinet will be drawer-over-door style. The opening between the upper and middle rail is 6". I am using $\frac{3}{4}$"-thick by $1\frac{1}{2}$"-wide oak hardwood to build the face frame. The frame's overall dimension equals the cabinet's width and height, or 16" wide by $26\frac{1}{4}$" high. Cut the frame parts to size and join the rails to the stiles, using glue and $1\frac{1}{4}$"-long pocket hole screws, in two pocket holes drilled on the back face of the frame rails.

4 Attach the face frame to the cabinet. The outside edges of the frame should be flush with the outside faces of the side and bottom boards, and aligned with the top edges of the side boards. You can use glue and biscuits, if you have a biscuit joiner, or nails. I am using 2" finishing nails and glue. The nail holes will be filled with a colored putty that matches the final finish of my cabinet. If you use this nail technique, be sure to drill pilot holes.

5 The base support frame can be made with solid wood or veneered sheet material. The exposed ends of base-frame ends G must be covered with edge tape if you use particleboard (PB) or plywood sheet material. The overall width of this frame is 4" narrower than the cabinet, leaving a 2" space on each side. The same 2" gap is left on the front and back, so the frame is 4" less than the cabinet depth. The 2" inset on the back will allow this cabinet to rest tight against a wall if you have baseboards installed in the room. The front space is for toe clearance, and the side inset is a style choice. Attach the frame to the underside of the cabinet, using glue and $1\frac{1}{4}$" pocket hole screws.

6 The top H for this cabinet is made with $\frac{3}{4}$"-thick veneer plywood edged with $1\frac{1}{2}$"-wide oak hardwood J and K. The top will be flush with the back of the cabinet and have a 1" overhang on the sides and front. The corners of this hardwood edging will be joined with 45° miters. Use glue and pocket hole screws to attach the hardwood edge. The top surfaces of the wood edging must be flush with the top face of H.

7 To secure the top, use right-angle metal brackets. They are installed flush with the top edges of the sides, backboard and face frame using ⅝"-long wood screws. Two brackets per side, back and front rail, will secure the top.

8 Before installing the top, round over the top and bottom edges. Leave the bottom face edge on the back square so it will cover the backboard's top edge. Use a ⅜"-radius router bit to ease the edges. Secure the top so it's flush with the back of the cabinet, leaving a 1" overhang on each side, using ⅝"-long screws in the brackets.

9 Spacer cleats L must be installed in the drawer area to support the bottom-mounted drawer glides. The inside edge of the face frame should be flush with the faces of these cleats. Use glue and 1¼"-long wood screws to install the cleats, aligning their bottom edges with the top edge of the middle rail.

10 In general, and for most common applications, the drawer box is 1" narrower and 1" less in height than the drawer opening in a cabinet. This is a general rule that applies to most bottom- and side-mounted drawer glides. My drawer box is made using $^{11}/_{16}$"-thick veneer PB; however, any sheet material is fine. The sides M are the total depth of the drawer box, and the front and back ends N are equal to the drawer-box width minus the thickness of the two sides. The bottom P equals the total drawer-box width and depth. The height of the sides M and ends N is equal to the total drawer-box height, minus the thickness of the bottom P. Cut the parts to size and apply wood veneer tape to the top edges of the sides, and ends, as well as to the side edges of the bottom. Join the ends N to the sides M with $1^{1}/_{4}$" pocket hole screws and glue. Secure the bottom P with glue and 2"-long PB screws. If the bottom has been cut square, the drawer box will be square.

11 I am using 18"-long drawer glides, which are actually $17^{3}/_{4}$" long. Install them according to the manufacturer's instructions. It's important that the cabinet runners for your drawer glide set are 90° to the face frame's front surface. Use a carpenter's square to draw screw lines at right angles to the frame's face. Set the drawer glide hardware $^{1}/_{8}$" back from the frame's front face and use $^{5}/_{8}$"-long screws to attach the drawer glide hardware.

DOOR CONSTRUCTION THEORY

A door being installed using European full-overlay hidden hinges is 1" wider than the inside opening of the cabinet. Since the face-frame stile-to-stile distance is smaller than the cabinet's interior, that is the dimension that will be used to calculate door width.

The inside stile-to-stile distance on this cabinet is 13", so the door must be 14" wide. Height isn't critical as long as the door covers the opening, but I want the lower rail of the face frame covered, and a $^{1}/_{2}$" overlap on the middle rail. That means my door height for this cabinet will be $17^{3}/_{4}$".

The frame-and-panel-style door is easy to make on a table saw. The door's stiles and rails are typically $2^{1}/_{4}$" wide, and $^{1}/_{4}$"-thick veneer plywood is used for the center panel.

Grooves are cut in the center of each stile and rail to accept the plywood panel. In this case, I've cut my grooves $^{3}/_{4}$" deep. Also, the rail ends have a tenon that's $^{1}/_{4}$" thick by $^{3}/_{4}$" long to fit in the rail grooves. Making a couple of passes over a standard table saw blade cuts the grooves. The tenons are cut on the table saw, as well, using a miter sled and a blade height of $^{1}/_{4}$". Make multiple passes with each rail on both faces until the tenon depth is achieved.

The drawer face is made using the same techniques as the door. However, I reduced the rail height to $1^{1}/_{2}$" because the drawer face is only 7" high and I didn't want a small center panel. Rail width reduction on drawer faces is common because of their small sizes.

12 Cut the grooves in each stile Q and rail R as detailed in "Door Construction Theory." Prepare all the parts listed for the door and drawer face. The tenons are ¼" thick and ¾" long to fit in the stile grooves.

13 Assemble the door and drawer face, using glue on the tenons only; don't glue the center panel. Clamp the joints until the adhesive sets. Sand both panels and round over the outside profile with a ⅜"-radius roundover router bit. If you don't own a router, ease the edges with a plane or sandpaper.

14 I will be mounting the door with two 107° full-overlay hidden hinges. These hinges require 35mm-diameter holes in the door, which are drilled ⅛" from the edge and 4" on center from each end. The depth of each hole is dependent on the hinge you are using, but typically the holes are ½" deep. Holes are bored with a flat-bottomed hinge-boring bit. Hinges and plates are normally sold separately because there are hundreds of combinations for different cabinet applications. In this case, I will be using the full-overlay hinge with a face-frame mounting plate. Face-frame hinge plates are used in this case because the stile-to-stile distance is less than the inside cabinet dimension, measuring inside face to inside face of the cabinet sides. The face-frame hinge plates mount directly on a stile edge with ⅝"-long wood screws. Predrill the stile edge before installing the hinge plate screws to avoid splitting the wood. Install the hinges and plates on the door, being sure to align the hinge flange parallel to the door edge. A square can be used to hold the hinge in proper alignment while it's secured in place with ⅝"-long wood screws.

15 Hold the door in its normally open position, with hinges and plates installed on the door. Verify that the bottom edge of the door is aligned with the bottom edge of the lower face-frame rail. I use a board clamped on the cabinet to hold the door in its proper position while I drive screws through the hinge plate holes and into the stile edge.

16 Once the door is correctly positioned, install the drawer face. It can be quickly and accurately aligned using a simple trick. First, decide on the type of handles or knobs that you are going to use. Drill the holes for the hardware in the drawer face only — not through the drawer box at this time. Use a spacer to align the drawer face on the cabinet. The spacer can be clamped in place or it can rest on the top edge of the door. Drive wood screws through the holes in the drawer face and into the drawer box. The wood screws will draw the face tightly against the drawer box and secure it in place. Now, carefully open the drawer and install four 1¼"-long wood screws through the back face of the drawer box front board and into the back of the drawer face. Remove the wood screws in the handle holes and install the pull hardware by drilling through the existing drawer face holes and drawer box. The result is a perfectly aligned drawer face every time.

CONSTRUCTION NOTES

This cabinet-building process has all the steps needed to build any size face-frame cabinet. The drawer-over-door style is common, but it can just as easily be constructed as a full-door or multi-drawer cabinet.

This project demonstrates the principles of face-frame and case joinery using pocket hole screws. It's just one joinery option that's available to all woodworkers. I used 1¹⁄₁₆"-thick veneer particleboard and ¾"-thick solid wood for my face frame. However, you can pick any material thickness or type that you'd prefer to use. The material choice is secondary; the main issue is the construction process.

This cabinet-building style can be used for kitchen and bathroom cabinetry, but I would suggest you use an adjustable shelf system by drilling columns of holes in the cabinet sides. This base can be fitted with a solid-wood top or a standard laminate roll-top.

This case joinery system can be used to build wall cabinets. You won't need a base frame, but you will have to add a top board, which is equal in dimensions to the bottom board, as wall cabinets do not have a countertop installed. In most applications, wall cabinets are 12" deep.

You may need a work center in your home. If so, two or three of these base units, built at 29¼" high with a ¾"-thick top, will be the perfect desk. File drawers are only larger versions of the drawer in this project. Build one of the bases with two large drawers and you'll have a great home office file center. Another unit with a full door and two adjustable shelves will give you plenty of room for all your office supplies. Finish your home office by building and installing a couple of wall units, using the same building techniques, and you're all set to tackle those home finances.

tall bookcase

ALMOST EVERYONE I KNOW COULD use another bookcase in his or her home. This project can be styled to fit any room, and would be a welcome addition as a storage or showcase cabinet for many items, including books. If you know a child who's an avid collector of things like dolls or racing cars, this is the perfect solution.

This bookcase is built using hidden pocket hole joinery. It's an extremely sturdy unit, which can support the weight of any normal collection. If you need to display unusually heavy items, I'll detail a support option that will increase the load capacity of the shelves.

The most important feature of this bookcase is the adjustable shelf system. You can build a fixed shelf version, but I think you'll find it limiting because all books aren't the same size. Adjustable shelves make this case suitable for any display items.

The project is made with veneer particleboard (PB) and readily available trim and solid wood. You don't need a fully equipped workshop to build this bookcase. A table saw, electric drills and a pocket hole jig are all the tools you'll need.

Once again, I'll follow my process of teaching the building techniques needed to build this project. The object isn't really to build this bookcase to the exact size shown; it's more about using the techniques to build one that meets your needs. The sizes stated are secondary to the process used to build the project.

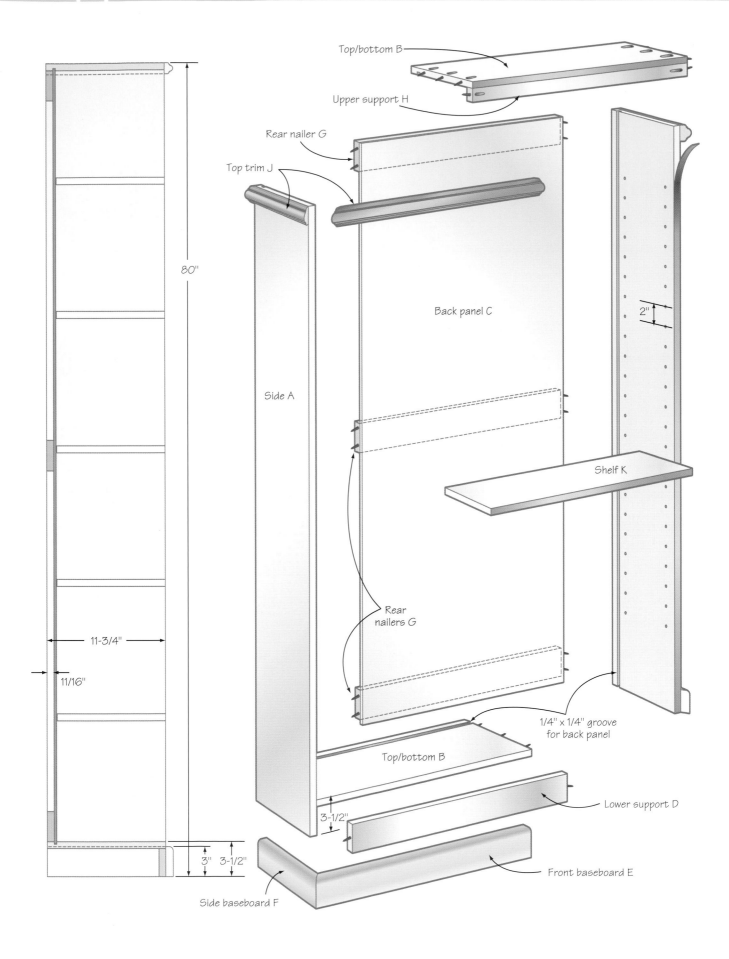

Top/bottom B

Upper support H

Rear nailer G

Top trim J

Back panel C

Side A

2"

Shelf K

Rear
nailers G

80"

11-3/4"

11/16"

1/4" x 1/4" groove
for back panel

Top/bottom B

Lower support D

3-1/2"

3" | 3-1/2"

Front baseboard E

Side baseboard F

inches (millimeters)

REFERENCE	QUANTITY	PART	STOCK	THICKNESS	(mm)	WIDTH	(mm)	LENGTH	(mm)	COMMENTS
A	2	sides	veneer PB	$^{11}/_{16}$	(18)	$11^3/_4$	(298)	80	(2032)	
B	2	top and bottom	veneer PB	$^{11}/_{16}$	(18)	$11^3/_4$	(298)	$28^5/_8$	(727)	
C	1	back panel	veneer ply	$^1/_4$	(6)	$29^1/_8$	(740)	$76^1/_8$	(1933)	
D	1	lower support	veneer PB	$^{11}/_{16}$	(18)	$2^{13}/_{16}$	(72)	$28^5/_8$	(727)	
E	1	front baseboard	hardwood	$^3/_4$	(19)	3	(76)	$31^1/_2$	(800)	
F	2	side baseboards	hardwood	$^3/_4$	(19)	3	(76)	$12^1/_2$	(318)	
G	3	rear nailers	veneer PB	$^{11}/_{16}$	(18)	3	(76)	$28^5/_8$	(727)	
H	1	upper support	veneer PB	$^{11}/_{16}$	(18)	$^{15}/_{16}$	(24)	$28^5/_8$	(727)	
J		top trim	hardwood					60	(1524)	
K	5	shelves	veneer PB	$^{11}/_{16}$	(18)	$10^3/_4$	(273)	$28^9/_{16}$	(725)	

Note: PB = particleboard.

hardware AND supplies

Pocket hole screws: $1^1/_4$" (32mm)

Wood screws: $1^1/_4$" (32mm)

Finishing nails

Glue

Shelf pins

Wood veneer edge tape

Wood putty

1 Cut the two sides A as well as the bottom and top B to the sizes indicated in the materials list. Form a $^1/_4$"-wide by $^1/_4$"-deep groove on the back, inside face of each panel. The back edge of each groove is $^{11}/_{16}$" away from the back edge of sides A to provide space for the rear nailers. Grooves can be cut on a table saw, but you will have to make two passes on each panel to achieve the required width. These grooves can also be cut with a $^1/_4$" straight router bit in a handheld or table-mounted router. Test fit a piece of the $^1/_4$" back panel to ensure the proper fit in all the grooves.

2 Adjustable shelf pin holes can be easily and accurately drilled using a shop-made jig. Cut a piece of sheet scrap that's 4" wide by 84" long. Attach to the top end a second piece of the same material that's 4" wide by 16" long, forming a T. Be sure to align the pieces at 90°. Drill a column of holes in the center of the jig, about 2" apart, that begins and ends 12" from the bottom and top. The column of holes should be drilled as accurately as possible. The drill bit diameter should suit the adjustable shelf pins you plan to use.

3 Mark the top of each side panel. The top of your jig is always placed at the top edge of the sides. Align the outside edge of the jig to the outside edge of the panel before drilling the column of holes. You'll need two columns on each side panel. Drill through the center of a dowel rod and place it on the bit, butted tight to the drill chuck to expose the length of drill bit needed for the required hole depth. You'll get properly placed holes at the correct depth using this jig method.

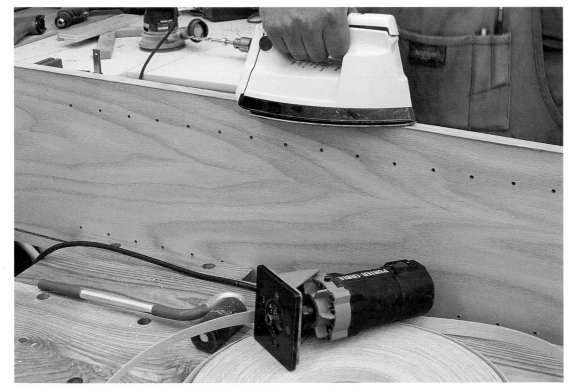

4 Apply matching edge tape to the front edges of the two sides A, top B and bottom B. I'm using oak veneer PB, so I will use preglued, iron-on wood-edge veneer tape.

shop TIP

Trimming wood veneer can be tricky because some of the wider grain woods, like oak, tend to tear along the grain pattern when using a knife or chisel. I use a flush-trim router bit to dress my wood edge. If you don't have a router, carefully use a sharp hand edge trimmer and sand the edges to make a clean edge.

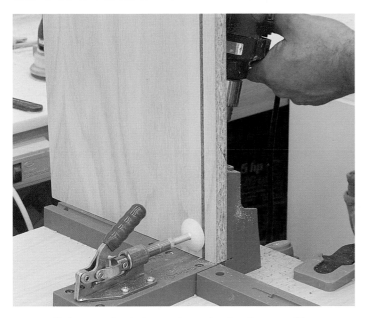

5 Drill three pocket holes on the ends of each top and bottom B. Both panels will have six pocket holes on the face opposite the groove.

6 Attach the top to the two sides; do not install the bottom at this time. Use 1¼"-long pocket hole screws and wood glue. The top face of this panel is aligned flush with the top edges of the side boards.

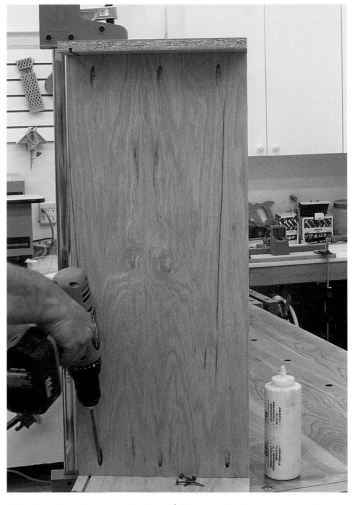

7 Cut the back panel C to the size shown in the materials list. Slip it into the side and top board grooves, using a small amount of glue to prevent back panel movement.

8 Install the bottom B using 1¼" pocket hole screws and glue. The back panel C will fit into the groove on the bottom board. Its top face is 3½" above the bottom edges of the side boards.

9 Cut and attach the lower support D. It's used to secure the bottom trim and strengthen the base of the bookcase. Use glue and 1¼" pocket hole screws to install this board. Its front face is aligned flush with the front edges of the side and bottom boards.

10 The base trim boards E and F are ¾"-thick hardwood, and installed flush with the bottom of sides A and lower support board D. Trim boards are installed with glue and 1¼"-long wood screws from the inside. The corners are joined with 45° miters. I am using a simple roundover technique on the top outside edges of my trim boards. However, any style of trim detailing can be done to match existing room furniture.

11 The three rear nailers G will support the back panel and allow you to anchor the cabinet to a wall if necessary. Attach them with pocket hole screws and glue, one at the top, bottom and center of the backboard.

12 The top trim J is a design element only, and can be omitted or changed to a style that suits your needs. I am using a bullnose-style trim that's available at most lumberyards. I will also install the support board H behind the upper trim. It's the same height as the trim, minus the thickness of the top board. Install this support board with glue and pocket hole screws in the front face, as it will be covered by the trim detail. If you are using particleboard or plywood for this support board, apply wood veneer tape to the bottom visible edge.

13 Attach the trim with glue and finishing nails, mitering the corners at 45°. You'll need about 5' of trim to cover the front and two sides.

14 If you require only four shelves, this project can be built with one sheet of $1\frac{1}{16}$"- or $\frac{3}{4}$"-thick material and two-thirds of a sheet of $\frac{1}{4}$" plywood veneer. If you need five shelves like I do, you'll have to buy a part sheet. Apply veneer tape to the front edges and install the shelves on pins. This bookcase was finished with three coats of satin polyurethane.

CONSTRUCTION NOTES

The important issue with this project is the building technique. I used dimensions that suit my room, but they can, and should be, changed to meet your needs. Change the height, width or depth, but I don't recommend building a unit that's wider than 36". If you need 5' of bookcase, I'd suggest you build two 30" units. Shelving boards wider than 36" tend to sag with weight.

Any type of sheet material could be used. If this bookcase will be used in your basement or storage shed, any inexpensive sheet material is suitable, and the top and bottom trim detail can be left off.

In the introduction, I mentioned shelf-load capacity because it's an important consideration. Shelves up to 30" long, like the ones in this bookcase, can support a reasonable mixture of books and collectibles. However, if you plan on shelving large, heavy volumes of books, you may want to consider using a $\frac{3}{4}$"-thick plywood material.

Installing a strong back can further strengthen shelves. A simple technique to increase the shelf-load capacity is to attach a $\frac{3}{4}$"-thick by $1\frac{1}{2}$"-high piece of hardwood on the lower back edge of the shelf. If that's not enough, the shelf capacity can be further increased by gluing a $\frac{3}{4}$"-thick by $1\frac{1}{2}$"-high hardwood edge on the front of each shelf in place of the veneer tape. The shelf boards will look thicker, but more importantly, the shelf capacity will be greatly increased.

notes

quilt rack

I DON'T KNOW A GREAT DEAL ABOUT making quilts, but I can appreciate how beautiful they are and how much work is lovingly done to create them. They should be on display, and this quilt rack can proudly show off three of your best.

I understand, based on my research, that these quilt racks were a common furniture item in bedrooms at one time. Before we had the luxury of central heat, it was often necessary to add a quilt or two to the bed to keep folks warm during cold winter nights. The quilts were stored on racks near the bed. They were more of a practical item in those days, but many people continue to use them as accent pieces in their homes.

If you are lucky enough to have a home with Colonial or rustic furniture, or any other appropriate decorative theme, this quilt rack will be a perfect fit. This rack was built for my mother-in-law, who is an avid quilter.

I was surprised to learn how popular quilting has become. There seems to be a club in every town and a great deal of activity about the hobby on the Internet. A simple Internet search yielded over 100,000 hits on the words *quilts* and *quilting*. PBS television produced a 60-minute documentary on the subject, describing the program as "selections from the 100 most acclaimed quilts of the 20th century." They traveled across America to meet the quilters in their homes and studios to discover the stories behind the creation of these magnificent treasures. It's a popular hobby with a long history, so you can see why this project will be a hit for your favorite quilter.

The quilt shown in the photograph is one of many, lovingly crafted by Elsie Lawrence of Prescott, Ontario. The care and attention to detail in her work is obvious.

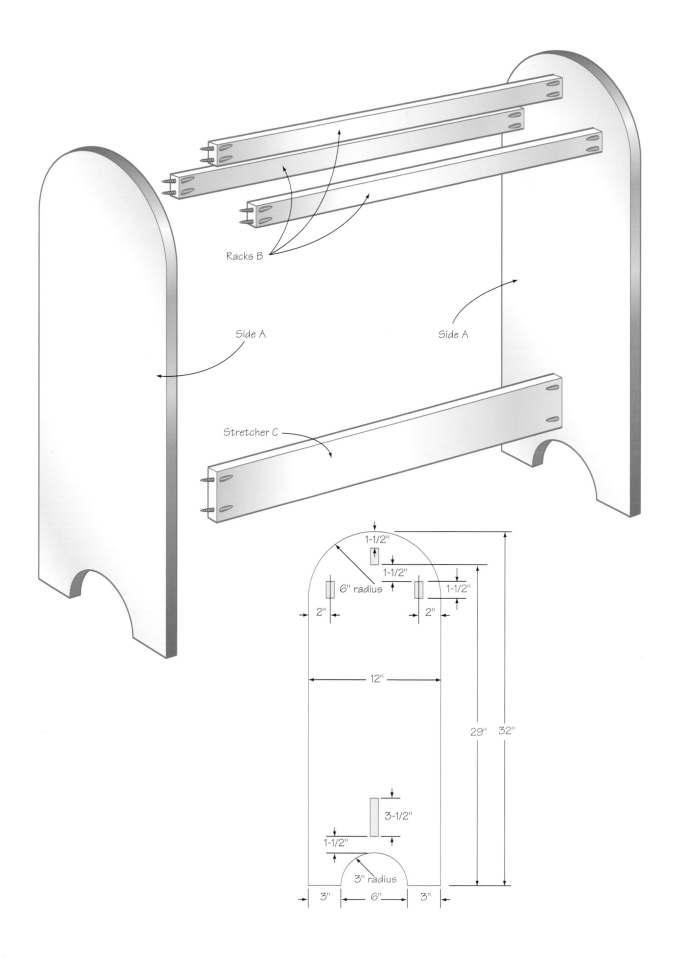

Racks B

Side A

Side A

Stretcher C

1-1/2"

1-1/2"

6" radius

1-1/2"

2"

2"

12"

29" 32"

3-1/2"

1-1/2"

3" radius

3"

6"

3"

inches (millimeters)

REFERENCE	QUANTITY	PART	STOCK	THICKNESS	(mm)	WIDTH	(mm)	LENGTH	(mm)	COMMENTS
A	2	sides	hardwood	³/₄	(19)	12	(305)	32	(813)	
B	3	racks	hardwood	³/₄	(19)	1¹/₂	(38)	31	(787)	
C	1	stretcher	hardwood	³/₄	(19)	3¹/₂	(89)	31	(787)	

hardware AND supplies

Pocket hole screws: 1¹/₄" (32mm)

Glue

Pocket hole plugs

1 Glue up enough boards to make the two rack sides A. I simply glue the edges and clamp the boards together until the adhesive sets. The edges can be prepared by cutting the boards on a well-tuned table saw, or, if you have a jointer, the edges can be dressed. If your table saw isn't accurate enough to rip the boards straight, or you don't own a jointer, your wood supplier will dress the edges for a small fee.

2 While the side panels are setting up, cut the three racks B and bottom stretcher C to the sizes indicated in the materials list. Drill two pocket holes on the ends of each board. These holes will be visible and filled with wood plugs, so space them equally on each board face.

3 Round over the four edges on the racks and stretcher boards, using a ¼"-radius router bit. Complete the sanding on these parts before assembly.

4 Clamp the two sides A together and draw a 6"-radius arc at one end (top) of the boards. Use a jigsaw to cut the arc. Keep the boards tightly clamped after cutting and sand both so the arcs are identical.

5 Draw a 3"-radius arc at the bottom center on each side panel. Cut the arc with a jigsaw and sand smooth. To complete the machine work on each side, round over all the edges, with the exception of the straight portion on the feet, using a ¼"-radius roundover bit.

6 Attach the three racks and one stretcher board to the sides with glue and 1¼" pocket hole screws. The racks are centered on the 2", 6" and 10" marks from the front edge of each side, as shown on the illustration. To align the racks, clamp a straight 1½"-wide board, with its top edge 29" from the bottom edge of the side. The center rack is aligned on top of the marker board, and the two outside racks are aligned on their marks below the marker board. The stretcher board is attached 1½" above the center of the lower arc on each side panel.

shop TIP

I discovered that screws buried a little deeper leave more room for the wood plugs. Set the stop collar on your bit about ⅛" higher than normal to achieve the extra hole depth.

A certain amount of tear is normal when drilling pocket holes. Often, the filler plugs have small gaps between them and the hole lines. To hide the damage, rub colored paste filler that matches your final finish into the edge where the wood plug meets the hole lines.

Once the colored filler paste dries, sand the area until the joint between the plug and hole outline is smooth and almost invisible. I discovered that a random-orbit sander was the best tool to sand the filled pocket holes.

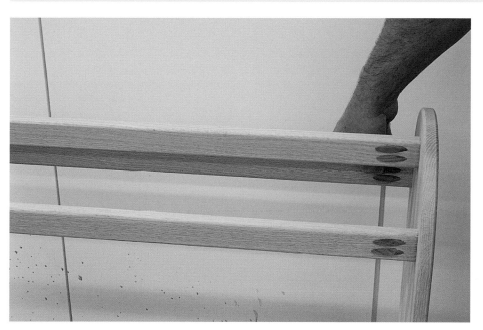

7 Install the pocket hole wood plugs, using glue. Once the adhesive is cured, sand the plugs smooth. Now you can apply your favorite finish to the rack.

construction NOTES

The choice of wood to use in this project is up to you. I encourage you to experiment with a few design changes and wood types.

As I was finishing this project, I realized that I missed using a design feature that would have added interest to the project. I could have joined the side boards with pocket holes and contrasting filler plugs, much like the rack and stretcher boards. If I had carefully cut my boards for the sides, taking into account the offset position of the pocket holes, I could have centered four plugs down the outside face of each panel.

I would have to place the pocket holes outside the waste area of each arc, but with a little planning, it would have been a nice-looking feature on my rack. I'll build the next rack with that technique.

notes

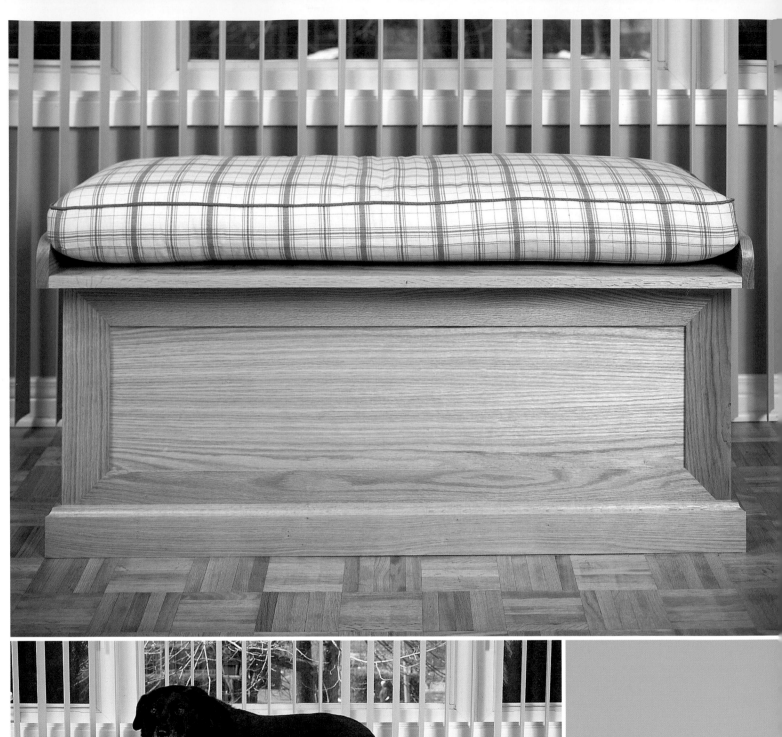

window bench

THIS WINDOW BENCH PROJECT would be a welcome addition to any room in your home. Build it for the living room and get extra seating, as well as storage for firewood; the children's room to provide a quiet place to stare out the window and store toys; or use it under a window in your bedroom and take advantage of the added storage for bed linens. This bench would also be a nice furniture accent piece at the foot of your bed.

I will be using my bench in the living room for extra seating and firewood storage, as I mentioned. However, it seems my dog has decided the bench was made for him to watch over his kingdom through our picture window. The cushion makes a great bed, and he's taken control of the bench, so there goes my extra seating solution.

I haven't installed panels on the inside of the box because I won't be storing anything of value. If you plan on using it for bed linens, or any other delicate items, you can install $\frac{1}{4}$"-thick veneer plywood panels, as I'll detail in the building steps.

I didn't realize how popular this window bench would be until I heard all the positive comments. It seems this project is on everyone's wish list, so I'll have to make a few more for family and friends. It's easy to build and simple to resize, so it can be custom built to meet any requirements.

Pocket hole joinery is perfect for this project. The frame-and-panel design is well suited to this joinery method, and the thick panels add a great deal of strength to the box. It should support a lot of weight.

The cushion is a piece of fabric covering a sheet of soft foam. The cover I used can be removed and washed, because I installed a zipper and purchased a machine-washable fabric. The seat pad is held in place with hook and loop fasteners so it won't move when someone sits down or the top is opened. Small strips of hook and loop fasteners can be purchased in any linen supply store.

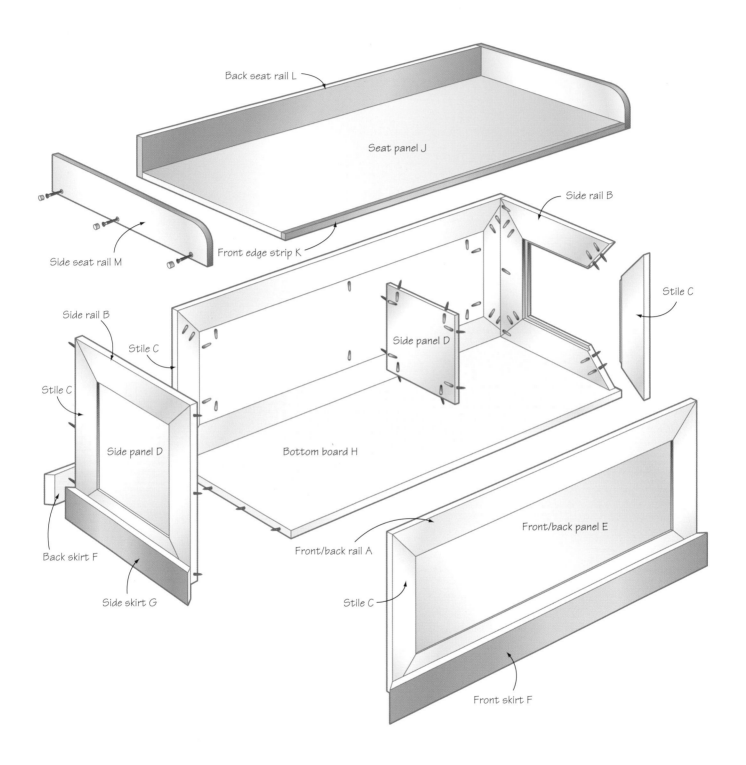

Back seat rail L

Seat panel J

Side seat rail M

Front edge strip K

Side rail B

Side rail B

Stile C

Stile C

Stile C

Side panel D

Side panel D

Bottom board H

Back skirt F

Side skirt G

Front/back rail A

Front/back panel E

Stile C

Front skirt F

inches (millimeters)

REFERENCE	QUANTITY	PART	STOCK	THICKNESS	(mm)	WIDTH	(mm)	LENGTH	(mm)	COMMENTS
A	4	front and back rails	solid wood	3/4	(19)	3	(76)	43	(1092)	mitered
B	4	side rails	solid wood	3/4	(19)	3	(76)	15	(381)	mitered
C	8	stiles	solid wood	3/4	(19)	3	(76)	15	(381)	mitered
D	2	side panels	veneer PB	1/2	(13)	10	(254)	10	(254)	
E	2	front and back panels	veneer PB	1/2	(13)	10	(254)	38	(965)	
F	2	front and back skirts	solid wood	3/4	(19)	3	(76)	44 1/2	(1131)	
G	2	side skirts	solid wood	3/4	(19)	3	(76)	18	(457)	
H	1	bottom board	particleboard	11/16	(18)	16 1/2	(419)	43	(1092)	
J	1	seat panel	particleboard	11/16	(18)	17 1/4	(438)	43 1/2	(1105)	
K	1	front edge strip	solid wood	11/16	(18)	1/2	(13)	43 1/2	(1105)	
L	1	back seat rail	solid wood	3/4	(19)	3	(76)	43 1/2	(1105)	
M	2	side seat rails	solid wood	3/4	(19)	3	(76)	18 1/2	(470)	

Note: PB = particleboard.

hardware AND supplies

	Pocket hole screws: 1 1/4" (32mm)
	Wood screws: 1 1/4" (32mm), 1 1/2" (38mm)
	PB screws: 2" (51mm)
	Brad nails
	Glue
3	No-mortise hinges
	Wood putty
	Wood plugs
	Seat fabric
	Seat foam
	Zipper
	Hook and loop fastener strips

1 Cut the four front and back rails A, the four side rails B and the eight stiles C about 1" longer than indicated in the materials list. That extra 1", at this point, will make it easier to machine the rabbets and leave enough room to miter the ends. Note that measurements for all rails and stiles are taken along the longest points of the miters. Next, set your table saw blade to cut a 1/2"-deep groove along one edge of each board. The outside edge of the cut should be 1/2" in from a face side.

2 The next cut, on the flat face of each board with the groove $\frac{1}{2}$" from that face, will form a rabbet that's $\frac{1}{2}$" wide by $\frac{1}{2}$" deep. The opposite face will have a $\frac{1}{4}$"-wide lip remaining.

3 After cutting the rabbets, each board needs a 45° miter on both ends. The rabbet should be along the shortest edge of the mitered boards. Then drill two pocket holes on both ends of each stile C (vertical member). These pocket holes are on the inside (rabbet) face of each stile, as shown.

4 Assemble the four frames, using $1\frac{1}{4}$"-long pocket hole screws and glue. The front and back frames should measure 15" high by 43" long, and the two side frames should be 15" high by 15" long. Because the pocket holes are closer to the inside edge of the miter, they tend to pull the miter apart on the outside edge. To prevent this, clamp the miters after installing the pocket hole screws and leave them until the adhesive cures.

shop TIP

I am not concerned about seeing the pocket holes, as mentioned in the introduction. However, if you want to hide the holes, there are wood plugs shaped for this purpose. Install them using glue, and sand the surface smooth once the adhesive sets.

5 The center panels D and E for the frames are $\frac{1}{2}$"-thick veneer particleboard. These panels are secured with $1\frac{1}{4}$" pocket hole screws and glue. Two screws on the 10"-long edge and three on the 38"-long edge will hold them securely. Remember to reset your pocket hole drill jig for $\frac{1}{2}$"-thick material.

6 The two end panels are joined to the front and back panels with glue and pocket hole screws. Drill three pocket holes on the vertical edges of each end panel, placing one at each end and one in the center.

8 The bottom board H is ¹¹⁄₁₆" veneer particleboard. Secure it to the bottom edges of the four panels, using glue and 1¹⁄₂"-long wood screws.

9 The seat panel J is also a piece of ¹¹⁄₁₆"-thick veneer particleboard. After installing the front edge strip, side and back rails, the seat will overhang each side by 1", and the front face of the bench by 2". I have aligned it flush with the back face of the box so I can install hinges. Cut the seat board J to the size shown in the materials list, and attach the ¹⁄₂"-thick strip K to the front edge, using glue and brad nails. Fill the nail holes with colored putty that matches your final finish and sand the strip smooth.

7 The base skirt is made using ³⁄₄"-thick by 3"-high hardwood. It's attached to the bottom of the side and end panels with glue and 1¹⁄₄"-long wood screws. The skirt boards are aligned 1" above the bottom edges of the box panels, and each corner is mitered. The measurements for skirt boards F and G are taken at the longest edge of the miter cuts. I used a cove router bit to profile the top, outside edges of my skirt boards.

10 The back rail L and side rails M will strengthen the seat and hold the cushion in place. The two side rails overlap the ends of the back rail. All seat rails are secured with glue and 2" particleboard screws in counterbored holes that are filled with wood plugs. Before installing the side rails, cut a smooth radius on the front top corners. This will remove the sharp corners and help to prevent injury if someone sits too close to either side rail. The seat rail bottom edges are aligned flush with the bottom face of seat board J.

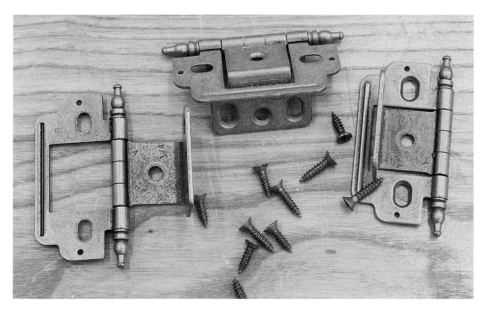

11 I'm using three no-mortise hinges to attach the seat to the box.

construction NOTES

I mentioned in the introduction that I would be using the window bench for firewood storage, so the interior doesn't require any further finishing. However, you can attach ¼"-thick veneer plywood panels to the inside faces of the sides, front and back frames with glue and brad nails. The top edge of the exposed plywood can be covered with small strips of moulding such as quarter-round.

Oak was my wood of choice, but any sheet material and hardwood combination could be used. Someone suggested poplar, which could be painted with contrasting colors on the panels and trim. A mix of light- and dark-colored woods could also be used.

Any of the dimensions could be altered to custom-fit your bench in a room. The bench size is dependent on window measurements, but keep in mind that normal seat height is about 18". This window bench can also be used as a coffee or sofa table by not installing the high side and back rails. Using large boxes or chests as coffee tables seems to be popular, and this design would be ideal for that application.

Material choices, as I mentioned, and final finishes can be just about any combination. My window bench is made of oak and has three coats of polyurethane to match my furniture. Experiment with a few different materials and paint finishes to find what's best for your bench.

chest of drawers

THE PROJECT IN THIS CHAPTER IS A chest of drawers, but again, it's a project that details construction procedures that can be applied to other pieces of furniture. Any type of case or carcass that has drawers can be built following the steps outlined in this chapter. However, this building style is best suited for bedroom chests and dressers.

I am using a combination of oak plywood and particleboard (PB) veneer sheet material. Sheet goods are stable, but the edges can be damaged, particularly in high-use areas such as the bedroom, so the top's perimeter and drawers have hardwood edges applied. This is a common technique that lowers the cost of construction, takes advantage of stable sheet material and gives the woodworker an opportunity to machine or profile the edges because of the applied hardwood.

Another common material is used to build the drawer boxes. Baltic birch, sometimes referred to as cabinet-grade plywood, is a favorite building material with many cabinetmakers. The multilayer colored edges

can be sanded smooth and left exposed because of the void-free properties of this material. Baltic birch is reasonably priced, stable and easy to use. Pocket hole screws, nails and glue are used to create strong joints with this material.

I'm taking advantage of modern hardware and using bottom-mounted drawer glides that attach to the cabinet sides and drawer boxes; no additional support frames are required. I'm also building the cabinet in a frameless style, which is an ideal application when low-cost, good-quality and sturdy case goods are required. These frameless-style cabinets may not be destined to become prized antiques, but they will serve you well for many years as good-quality cabinets for any room in your home. They are a cost-effective solution for the guest room or child's bedroom.

This chest of drawers is 30" wide by 48" high and 19" deep. However, you can make it any size you require, and I discuss the options in the Construction Notes at the end of this chapter.

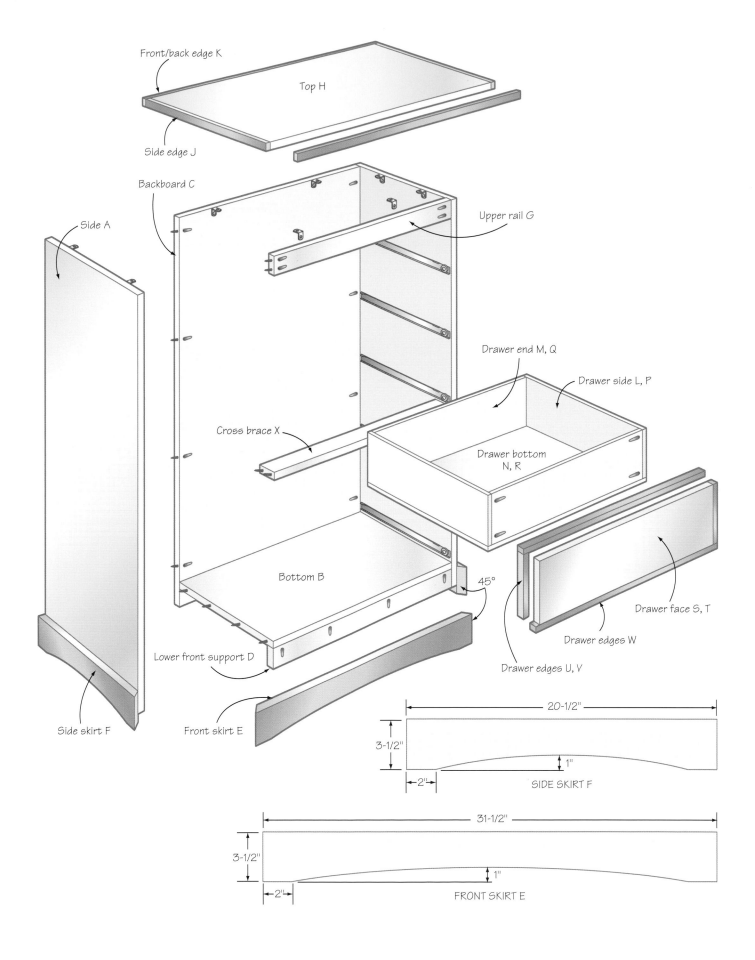

Front/back edge K

Top H

Side edge J

Backboard C

Side A

Upper rail G

Drawer end M, Q

Drawer side L, P

Cross brace X

Drawer bottom N, R

Bottom B

45°

Drawer face S, T

Drawer edges W

Lower front support D

Drawer edges U, V

Side skirt F

Front skirt E

20-1/2"

3-1/2"

1"

2"

SIDE SKIRT F

31-1/2"

3-1/2"

1"

2"

FRONT SKIRT E

inches (millimeters)

REFERENCE	QUANTITY	PART	STOCK	THICKNESS	(mm)	WIDTH	(mm)	LENGTH	(mm)	COMMENTS
A	2	sides	veneer ply	3/4	(19)	19	(483)	46	(1168)	
B	1	bottom	veneer ply	3/4	(19)	19	(483)	28 1/2	(724)	
C	1	backboard	veneer PB	3/4	(19)	28 1/2	(724)	43 1/4	(1098)	
D	1	lower front support	veneer ply	3/4	(19)	2	(51)	28 1/2	(724)	
E	1	front skirt	hardwood	3/4	(19)	3 1/2	(89)	31 1/2	(800)	
F	2	side skirts	hardwood	3/4	(19)	3 1/2	(89)	20 1/2	(521)	
G	1	upper rail	hardwood	3/4	(19)	1 1/2	(38)	28 1/2	(724)	
H	1	top	veneer ply	3/4	(19)	19	(483)	31	(787)	
J	2	side edges	hardwood	3/4	(19)	1/2	(13)	19	(483)	
K	2	front and back edges	hardwood	3/4	(19)	1/2	(13)	32	(813)	
L	8	drawer sides	Baltic birch	1/2	(13)	5	(127)	18	(457)	
M	8	drawer ends	Baltic birch	1/2	(13)	5	(127)	26 1/2	(673)	
N	4	drawer bottoms	Baltic birch	1/2	(13)	18	(457)	27 1/2	(699)	
P	2	drawer sides	Baltic birch	1/2	(13)	8 3/4	(222)	18	(457)	
Q	2	drawer ends	Baltic birch	1/2	(13)	8 3/4	(222)	26 1/2	(673)	
R	1	drawer bottom	Baltic birch	1/2	(13)	18	(457)	27 1/2	(699)	
S	4	drawer faces	veneer ply	3/4	(19)	7	(178)	28 3/4	(730)	
T	1	drawer face	veneer ply	3/4	(19)	9 3/4	(248)	28 3/4	(730)	
U	2	drawer edges	hardwood	3/4	(19)	1/2	(13)	9 3/4	(248)	
V	8	drawer edges	hardwood	3/4	(19)	1/2	(13)	7	(178)	
W	10	drawer edges	hardwood	3/4	(19)	1/2	(13)	29 3/4	(756)	
X	1	cross brace	hardwood	3/4	(19)	1 1/2	(38)	28 1/2	(724)	

hardware AND supplies

Pocket hole screws: 1 1/4" (32mm), 1" (25mm)

Wood screws: 5/8" (16mm), 1" (25mm)

Brad nails

Glue

Iron-on wood veneer tape

Right-angle brackets

Wood putty

Drawer glides

Drawer pulls

1 Cut the two sides A and bottom B as listed in the materials list. Apply iron-on wood veneer tape to the front edges of all three panels. Then drill four pocket holes on each side of the bottom board. The holes are drilled on the underside of panel B.

2 Join the bottom B to the sides A with glue and 1¼" pocket hole screws. Align panel B so its bottom face is 2" above the ends of each side board.

shop TIP

The backboard panel won't be visible, so it can be any $^{11}/_{16}$"- or $^3/_4$"-thick piece of material that you have in your shop. Veneer plywood is expensive, so this is a good place to substitute a less costly material.

3 Cut the backboard C to the size indicated in the materials list, and drill pocket holes on the inside face of the sides. Install this panel with $1^1/_4$" pocket hole screws and glue. Its back face is aligned flush with the back edges of the side and bottom boards.

The hardwood skirt board arcs can be cut to the dimensions indicated by using a simple technique. First, drive finishing nails on the waste side of the arc to be cut at the center and both ends. Then, bend a thin strip of hardwood around the nails to form the desired arc. Clamp the ends and trace the arc using the hardwood strip as a guide.

4 The lower front support D is used to strengthen the cabinet base and provide a surface to glue and attach the front skirt board. Install the support board with glue and $1\frac{1}{4}$" pocket hole screws on the front face, as the skirt board will cover it. Its front face should be flush with the front edges of the side and bottom boards.

5 The front and side skirts E and F are mitered at 45°. They are $\frac{3}{4}$"-thick hardwood with an arc cut on the lower edge of each piece. Round over the top edges of each piece, using a $\frac{3}{8}$"-radius bit in your router, before cutting the miters. These boards are attached to the cabinet carcass with their top edges $2\frac{1}{8}$" above the bottom ends of the side and lower support boards. That position will hide the lower front support D to bottom B joint.

6 Before taking the cabinet off your bench, use a ⅜"-radius bit in a router to soften the lower edges of the front and side skirt boards.

7 The upper rail G is attached to the sides with 1¼"-long pocket hole screws and glue on the back face. Align the top edge of this rail with the top edges of the sides A.

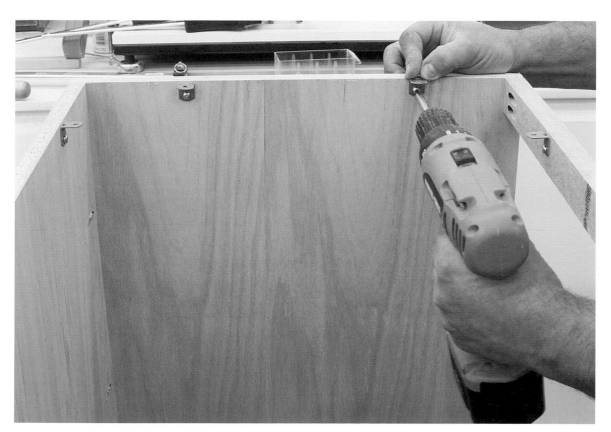

8 The top H will be attached to the cabinet using ⅝"-long screws in right-angle metal brackets. Install two brackets on the sides, backboard and back face of the front rail.

9 I will be using a wood edge technique for the cabinet top and drawer faces. Thin strips of ½"-thick wood are attached to all edges with glue and brad nails. As mentioned previously, this technique is a lot less expensive when compared to using solid wood, and it allows the woodworker to profile the panel edges. The top will be 20" deep and 32" wide. The ¾"-thick veneer plywood or PB is 19" deep by 31" wide with ½"-wide strips of hardwood on each edge to achieve the final size. Cut and attach the wood strips J and K. The final size is needed so the top will overhang each side and the front edge of the cabinet by 1", and align flush with the back face.

10 Fill the nail holes with colored putty to match the final finish of your cabinet. Sand the edges and round over the top and bottom face edges of the top with a ⅜"-radius bit. Don't round over the rear, bottom edge, as it will align flush with the back of the cabinet.

11 Attach the cabinet top, using ⅝"-long wood screws through the brackets. Align the top H with the required overhang as detailed in step 9.

CALCULATING DRAWER BOX HEIGHTS IN FRAMELESS CABINETS

This chest of drawers is a frameless-style cabinet with about 41¾" of free space for drawer boxes. Free space is the open area in a cabinet that can be used for drawer boxes.

Generally, drawer boxes require 1" of clearance above and below the box. Between drawer boxes there should be a 2" space, as well as 1" of space above the top box and 1" below the bottom box. However, the bottom box free space can be filled with the cabinet's baseboard because there would be nothing but space and it's not required to remove or operate the drawer box. This is a general rule,

and leaves extra room for a little adjusting if required.

This chest of drawers has about 41¾" of open area, which includes a part of the bottom board thickness. I've installed five drawer boxes, which means I need a total of 10" of clearance (2" between each box and 1" above the top, as well as 1" below the bottom drawer) that can't be used for drawers. Subtract the 10" hardware clearance from the free space height of 41¾" and we are left with 31¾". This remaining space can be occupied by any total height of five drawer boxes.

In this project I've reduced the bottom drawer box height by ½" to get a little more space.

Drawer faces can be roughly calculated at a height of 2" greater than the drawer box for material estimation purposes. However, the easiest method is to install the drawer boxes and measure the drawer face heights needed on the cabinet. The drawer height sizes may have to be altered slightly for a visual balance of the faces. After I installed the drawer boxes, I tried a few combinations and arrived at the sizes shown in the material list.

12 Drawer boxes are 1" narrower than the cabinet's interior dimension for most drawer glide hardware. Check the specifications of your hardware before cutting the box parts. The drawer boxes are constructed using ½"-thick Baltic birch plywood. The drawer ends are attached to the drawer sides with 1" pocket hole screws and glue. The bottom drawer box is 27½" wide by 9¼" high, and the four remaining boxes are 27½" wide by 5½" high. All the drawer boxes are 18" deep. Drill the pocket holes, remembering to reset your pocket hole jig for ½" material, and assemble the parts.

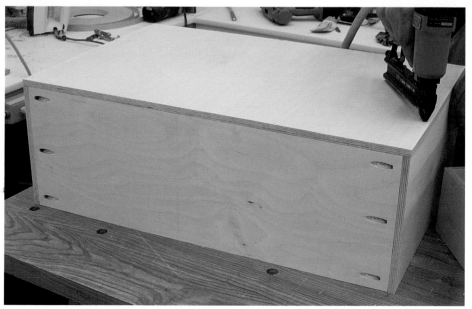

13 Attach the drawer bottoms with glue and brad nails. Align the four panels of each box to the edges of the bottom to square the drawer. If the bottom was cut square, the completed drawer box will be square.

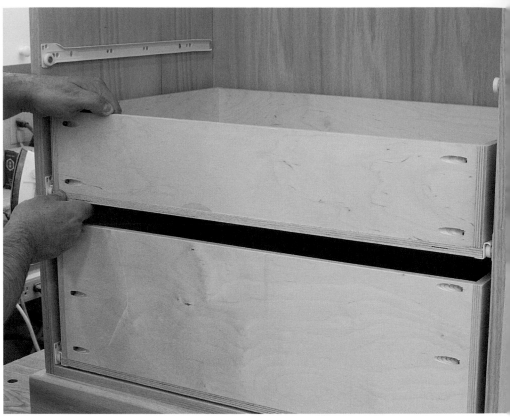

14 The drawer-box bottoms should be aligned at the 0", 11", 19", 27" and 35" marks on the cabinet's interior exposed faces. The measurement begins at the bottom board of the cabinet. A simple way to mark each side panel equally is to use a story stick, as shown. The cabinet runner portions of your drawer glide sets can be attached with ⅝"-long wood screws to the side panels. Be sure to align the drawer runners so the bottom edges of the boxes are at the correct location. The runners should be ⅛" behind the cabinet's front edge.

15 Install the cabinet runners, using a carpenter's square as a guide. The runners should be at a 90° angle to the cabinet's front edge. Attach the drawer-box runners following the manufacturer's specifications and test fit the drawers.

16 The bottom drawer face is 10¾" high, and the remaining four faces are 8" high. They are all 29¾" wide. The drawer faces are made with ¾"-thick veneer plywood or PB. All the edges have a ½"-wide strip of hardwood attached following the same process as the top board. Before installing the drawer faces, round over the front face edges on all the panels.

17 The sides of tall frameless cabinets, such as this chest, could flex if heavy loads were placed in the drawer boxes. To prevent this movement, I install a cross brace after the drawer glide runners are located. It's installed directly under a set of cabinet runners, as close to the middle of the cabinet as possible. The brace won't be seen once the drawer faces are installed. Use glue and two 1¼" pocket hole screws on each end to attach the cross brace X to the cabinet sides.

18 Install the drawer faces with a ⅛" space between each. I always drill my handle or knob holes in the drawer faces and use these holes to drive screws into the box to temporarily secure the face once it has been properly aligned. Then I pull out the drawer, with the face attached, and drive four 1"-long screws through the back side of the front boards and into the rear of the drawer face. Once that is complete, I remove the handle hole screws, drill completely through the box front board and install the drawer handles or knobs.

kitchen display
AND storage cabinet

I NAMED THIS PROJECT A KITCHEN Display and Storage Cabinet, but soon realized that it could be used in many areas of your home. It's ideal as a sideboard and added storage center in a large kitchen, as I originally intended, but it can also be a useful piece of furniture in a small dining room. The center can be used as an addition to your existing buffet and hutch, or as the primary cabinet when space is at a premium.

Someone suggested that it would be a great refreshment storage and service cabinet for the family room. And another person said they'd use it for a basement apartment eat-in kitchen they were building in their home. I had all kinds of suggested uses, which tells me a great deal about the usefulness of this project.

The angled breakfront on the base is a feature that really makes this a unique piece. The cabinet appears to be complex, requiring complicated construction techniques, but is surprisingly simple to build thanks to pocket hole joinery. Traditional angle joinery requires that each part be half the final angle

to form the joint. Pocket hole joinery, on the other hand, uses one straight member and a full-angle cut on the joining piece to achieve the required angle.

This unique joining method puts the intersection of both pieces slightly off the angled point, where the joint turns, leaving a crisp corner seam. The line where both pieces are joined is on a flat surface, and not the point, so the joint virtually disappears. It's a lot of fun to experiment with these angled joints using pocket hole joinery, and it opens up a lot of interesting possibilities.

I've done a bit of experimenting with different pocket hole applications in this project, so check out all the techniques and pick a few that work best for you. A note of caution though — this isn't an inexpensive project! The cost of hardwood, veneer plywood, hardware and glass add up quickly, and spending upwards of $300 isn't out of the question. However, you would have difficulty finding a store-bought piece, similar in quality to this project, at that price.

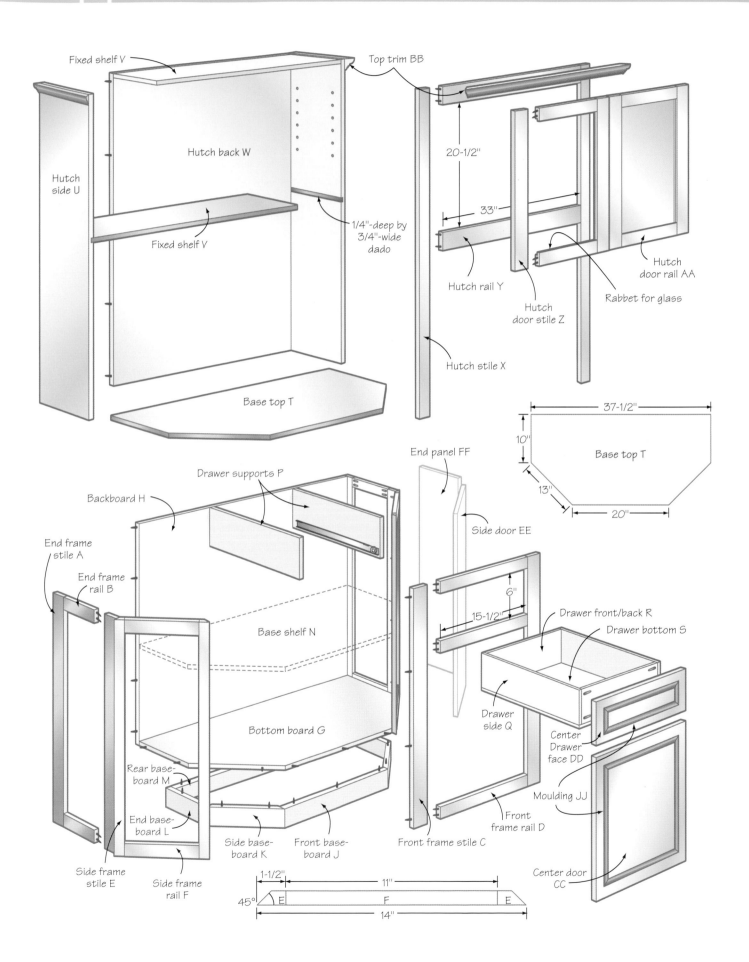

Fixed shelf V

Top trim BB

Hutch back W

Hutch side U

Fixed shelf V

1/4"-deep by 3/4"-wide dado

20-1/2"

33"

Hutch rail Y

Hutch door stile Z

Rabbet for glass

Hutch door rail AA

Hutch stile X

Base top T

37-1/2"

10"

Base top T

13"

20"

End panel FF

Drawer supports P

Backboard H

Side door EE

End frame stile A

End frame rail B

Base shelf N

6"

15-1/2"

Drawer front/back R

Drawer bottom S

Drawer side Q

Bottom board G

Center Drawer face DD

Rear base-board M

Moulding JJ

End base-board L

Front frame rail D

Center door CC

Side frame stile E

Side base-board K

Front base-board J

Front frame stile C

Side frame rail F

1-1/2"

45° E

11"

F

E

14"

inches (millimeters)

REFERENCE	QUANTITY	PART	STOCK	THICKNESS	(mm)	WIDTH	(mm)	LENGTH	(mm)	COMMENTS
A	4	end frame stiles	hardwood	3/4	(19)	1 1/2	(38)	30	(762)	
B	4	end frame rails	hardwood	3/4	(19)	1 1/2	(38)	7	(178)	
C	2	front frame stiles	hardwood	3/4	(19)	2 1/4	(57)	30	(762)	
D	3	front frame rails	hardwood	3/4	(19)	1 1/2	(38)	15 1/2	(394)	
E	4	side frame stiles	hardwood	3/4	(19)	1 1/2	(38)	30	(762)	angled
F	4	side frame rails	hardwood	3/4	(19)	1 1/2	(38)	11	(279)	
G	1	bottom board	veneer ply	3/4	(19)	18	(457)	37 1/2	(953)	
H	1	backboard	veneer ply	3/4	(19)	30	(762)	37 1/2	(953)	
J	1	front baseboard	veneer ply	3/4	(19)	4	(102)	19	(483)	
K	2	side baseboards	veneer ply	3/4	(19)	4	(102)	11 1/4	(285)	
L	2	end baseboards	veneer ply	3/4	(19)	4	(102)	7 1/2	(191)	
M	1	rear baseboard	veneer ply	3/4	(19)	4	(102)	33 3/4	(857)	
N	1	base shelf	veneer ply	3/4	(19)	17 7/8	(454)	37 3/8	(950)	angled
P	2	drawer supports	veneer ply	3/4	(19)	7 1/2	(191)	18	(457)	
Q	2	drawer sides	Baltic birch ply	1/2	(13)	4 1/2	(115)	18	(457)	
R	2	drawer back and front	Baltic birch ply	1/2	(13)	4 1/2	(115)	13 1/2	(343)	
S	1	drawer bottom	Baltic birch ply	1/2	(13)	14 1/2	(369)	18	(457)	
T	1	base top	hardwood	3/4	(19)	20 1/2	(521)	41	(1041)	angled
U	2	hutch sides	veneer ply	3/4	(19)	9 1/4	(235)	42	(1067)	
V	2	hutch fixed shelves	veneer ply	3/4	(19)	8 1/2	(216)	35	(889)	
W	1	hutch back	veneer ply	3/4	(19)	34 1/2	(877)	42	(1067)	
X	2	hutch stiles	hardwood	3/4	(19)	1 1/2	(38)	42	(1067)	
Y	2	hutch rails	hardwood	3/4	(19)	3 1/2	(89)	33	(838)	
Z	4	hutch door stiles	hardwood	3/4	(19)	2 1/4	(57)	22	(559)	
AA	4	hutch door rails	hardwood	3/4	(19)	2 1/4	(57)	12 1/2	(318)	
BB		top trim	hardwood					6'	(2m)	
CC	1	center door	veneer ply	3/4	(19)	16 1/2	(419)	21 1/2	(546)	
DD	1	center drawer face	veneer ply	3/4	(19)	16 1/2	(419)	7 1/2	(191)	
EE	2	side doors	veneer ply	3/4	(19)	12	(305)	29 1/2	(750)	
FF	2	end panels	veneer ply	3/4	(19)	8	(203)	29 1/2	(750)	
GG	2	hutch door panels	glass	1/8	(3)	13 1/8	(333)	18 1/8	(460)	
HH	1	hutch shelf	glass	1/4	(6)	8 1/4	(209)	34 3/8	(874)	
JJ		moulding						40'	(12m)	cut to fit doors and panels

hardware AND supplies

Pocket hole screws: 1 1/4" (32mm), 1 1/4" (32mm), 1" (25mm)	Right-angle metal brackets
Wood screws: 2" (51mm), 5/8" (16mm), 1" (25mm), 1 1/4" (32mm)	Wood putty
Brad nails	Pocket hole plugs
Finishing nails	Glass clips
Glue	10" (254mm) door hinges
Shelf pins	Handles
Wood veneer edge tape	Cabinet lights
18" (457mm) full-extension drawer glides	

1 Begin the project by constructing the face frames. The two 10"-wide by 30"-high end frames are built with parts A and B. Use glue and two 1¼" hardwood pocket hole screws at each joint.

2 The single front frame is built with the 2¼"-wide stiles C and the 1½"-wide rails D. The extra stile width is required to conceal the pocket holes that are drilled on the rear faces to join the middle frame to the side frames. A third rail is installed in this frame, leaving a 6"-high opening below the top rail for the drawer box. Assemble this 20"-wide by 30"-high front frame with two 1¼" pocket hole screws and glue at each joint.

3 The two side frames require 45° cuts on the outside edges of all stiles. The front faces of the four stiles E, after ripping the angles, are 1½" wide. Unlike traditional joinery, a 45° joint using pocket holes is achieved by cutting the full angle on only one of the pieces to be joined. Join the rails F to the angled stiles E with glue and 1¼" pocket hole screws to form two side frames that are 14" wide, measured on the front face, by 30" high.

4 Before joining the frames, two drilling steps are needed. First, a column of adjustable shelf pin holes should be drilled. The holes are located on the back faces of the two forward stiles on both end frames, and the back faces of each front frame stile. I'm using a shop-made jig, which is built using a flat steel bar with equally spaced drilled holes and a plywood base with hardwood supports.

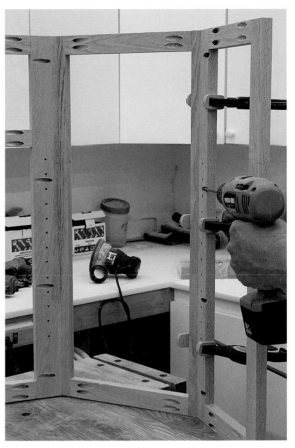

5 Drill pocket holes in the forward stile (stile closest to the cabinet front) on each end frame. These will be used to join the end frames to the side frames. Four holes in each stile will be enough to secure the frames. Pocket holes on the back face of these 1½"-wide stiles will partially tear the edge. However, fixed end panels will hide the tears.

6 Drill four pocket holes on both rear faces of the front frame stiles. They will be used to join the front frame to the two side frames. Join the five frames with glue and 1¼" pocket hole screws. All the back faces of the stiles should be in line at the outside corners. A small part of the 45° angled rip on the side frame stiles will extend past the faces of the end and middle frames. This excess will be removed in the next step.

7 Remove the excess angled rip material on the side frames, using a plane or belt sander. Sand all the front faces smooth before proceeding.

8 Block the frame by attaching a temporary strap to the back edges of the end frames. Check that all frame-to-frame joints are at 45°. If not, use clamps and wedges cut at 45° to hold the frame in its proper position. The end frames should also be parallel to each other. My inside frame-to-frame dimension is 37½", which may be slightly different from yours, due to cutting and assembly procedures. Create a template of the inside perimeter of the frame, using a thin sheet of plywood or hardboard, and cut it to size. The template will be used to lay out the bottom board G, base shelf N and top T.

9 Use the template to mark the bottom board G. The depth (front to back edge) of the bottom is shortened by ¾" to leave room for the backboard H. Drill pocket holes on the underside of the bottom board for screws that will secure it to the face-frame assembly. The bottom board is attached with 1¼" pocket hole screws and glue, and has its bottom edge aligned flush with the bottom edges of the face frames.

10 The backboard H is also ¾"-thick veneer plywood. Before installing, drill two columns of shelf pin holes in the front face that are aligned with the previously drilled holes in the stiles. The hole columns are located about 10" from each end of this panel. The backboard overlaps the bottom board and is secured with glue and 2" wood screws. Pocket holes on the rear face are used to attach it to each stile of the back frames.

11 The base frame is constructed using $\frac{3}{4}$"-thick veneer plywood with parts J, K, L and M. All corners are mitered at 45° by cutting each part at $22\frac{1}{2}$°, with the exception of the rear baseboard M, which is a straight butt joint. Drill pocket holes on the inside face of each board and secure them to the bottom board with $1\frac{1}{4}$" pocket hole screws and glue. Use glue and brad nails at each miter to keep the intersecting joints tight. The frame members are set 2" back from the cabinet face on all edges, including the back face. This 2" setback will provide toe room at the front and sides, and allow the cabinet to rest tight to the wall at the back, because it will be higher than standard wall base trim.

12 Use the template to draw an outline on $\frac{3}{4}$" veneer plywood for an adjustable base shelf N. It should be reduced by $\frac{1}{16}$" on the end, side and front edges, as well as a $\frac{3}{4}$" reduction on the back edge, so it can be moved easily in the cabinet. Apply iron-on heat-sensitive adhesive wood veneer tape to the end, side and front edges of this shelf board.

13 Cut the two drawer supports P. They are attached to the back faces of the middle frame stiles and the backboard. Use $1\frac{1}{4}$" pocket hole screws and glue on the front ends and wood screws through the backboard at the rear. Carefully align these support panels so they are flush with the inside edges of the middle frame stiles at the drawer opening. The supports must be parallel to each other and at 90° on the backboard. Use a carpenter's square to draw position lines on the backboard.

14 The drawer box opening is 6" high by $15\frac{1}{2}$" wide and $18\frac{3}{4}$" deep, so I will build an 18"-deep drawer box. The drawer box is 1" narrower than the opening, and 1" less in height to accommodate the full-extension side-mounted glides that I used. The box is made using $\frac{1}{2}$"-thick Baltic birch, sometimes referred to as cabinet-grade plywood. The sides Q are joined to the front and back R with 1" pocket hole screws and glue. The bottom S is secured with glue and brad nails. The overall dimension of the drawer box is 5" high by $14\frac{1}{2}$" wide and 18" deep.

15 Install the drawer glides following the manufacturer's instructions. As mentioned, I'm using full-extension glides, but standard, less-expensive three-quarter-extension drawer glides can be used.

16 The top T is made using solid wood by gluing up a series of ¾"-thick boards. Join the boards using pocket hole joinery and glue. But pay special attention to the placement of the pocket holes, because the top will be cut using the template as a guide. The boards can be edge dressed on a jointer or cut parallel on a well-tuned table saw. If you don't have the equipment, have your lumber supplier dress the edges on their jointer. The charges at most lumberyards for this service are usually reasonable. Once the adhesive has set, cut the top using the template, but add 1" to the ends, sides and front edges. The back is cut to the template dimension so that edge will be flush with the back edge of the cabinet.

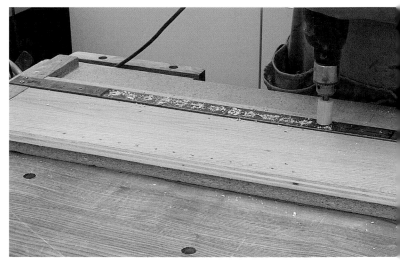

17 The top is secured to the cabinet using right-angle metal brackets and ⅝"-long wood screws. I made the holes in these brackets larger to allow some room for expansion and contraction of the solid-wood top. The enlarged holes are twice the diameter of the screw shaft that I used. Round over the top and bottom edges of the top, using a ¼"-radius roundover bit in a router, but leave the back edge square. Attach the top so there's a 1" overhang on all faces of the cabinet and it is flush with the outside face of the backboard.

18 The two hutch sides U are ¾"-thick veneer plywood. Drill adjustable shelf pin holes in the top 20" of each side panel, because the upper section will have a fixed shelf at the 24" mark. Keep the rear column of holes 2" away from the back edge of each side to leave room for the ¾"-thick hutch back.

19 Use a router with a straight-cutting bit or a table saw with a dado blade to cut a ¾"-wide rabbet on the top edge of both side boards. The same setup can be used to cut a ¾"-wide dado on the inside face of each board. These dadoes are 24" below the top edge of each side, measured to the top edge of the dado cut. Both rabbets and dadoes are ¼" deep. If you're using a router, clamp the two sides together to ensure the cuts will be perfectly aligned.

20 The hutch is 36" wide, measured on the outside faces. Two fixed ¾"-thick veneer plywood shelves V are installed in the rabbets and dadoes and secured with glue. Clamp the assembly until the glue sets. The shelves V are ¾" narrower than the sides U. They are installed flush with the front edges of the sides U to leave a ¾"-wide space at the rear for the back.

21 Cut the hutch back W and drill a column of shelf pin holes at the center point to align with the holes in the side boards. The back is attached to the sides using 1¼" pocket hole screws, and to the fixed shelves with 2"-long wood screws and glue on all edges. This full-thickness back will add strength and weight to the hutch, as well as square up the carcass.

22 The hutch face frame is built using 1½"-wide stiles X and 3½"-wide rails Y. Both rail top edges are aligned flush with the upper surfaces of the two fixed shelves. These wide rails will be used to hide light fixtures in the upper and lower sections of the hutch. Attach the rails to the stiles with 1¼" pocket hole screws on the rear face of both rails.

23 Attach the face frame to the hutch carcass with glue and finishing nails. Fill the nail holes with colored putty that matches the cabinet's final finish color. If you prefer, you can attach the face frame using biscuit joinery if you have the equipment.

24 Purchase the top trim moulding BB at this point and mark its position on the cabinet. Use a ¼"-radius roundover bit in a router and ease the outside edges of each stile up to the lower edge of the top trim. Leave the area under the trim moulding square, so it will rest flat on the cabinet frame. Round over the inside edges of the lower section stiles and rails, using the same bit.

shop TIP

I'm using standard 107° hidden hinges with a special plate. Standard hinge plates are typically attached to the cabinet side board. However, this hutch carcass has a face frame that extends past the inside face of the side boards, meaning a standard plate cannot be installed. A special face-frame mounting plate is used for this application, and is attached to the inside edges of each stile, using ⅝"- or ¾"-long wood screws.

25 The upper opening is 33" wide by 20½" high. The doors will be a frame style with tempered glass center panels. They will be mounted using European hidden hinges and face-frame mounting plates. To calculate the width of each door, add 1" to the opening width and divide by two. Using that formula means I will need two 17"-wide doors (33" + 1" = 34" divided by 2). They will be 22" high to provide a ¾" overlap on the upper and lower rails. The doors are made using 2¼"-wide stiles Z and 2¼"-wide rails AA. They are joined with two 1¼" pocket hole screws and glue at each corner. Drill these pocket holes about ⅛" deeper than standard, as we will be filling them with wood plugs. Keep the pocket holes together and as close to the outside edge as possible to provide room for a rabbet cut that will hold the center tempered glass panel.

26 Fill the pocket holes with wood plugs that match the wood type you are using. Round over the front inner and outer perimeter, using a ¼"-radius router bit.

27 Use a rabbeting bit in your router to form a ⅛"-deep cut on the inside back perimeter of the frame for the tempered glass panel GG. Square the corners and order the size of tempered glass required to fit your rabbet cut. Use small plastic clips and ⅝"-long wood screws to hold the glass securely.

29 The base center door CC, center drawer face DD, two side doors EE and two end panels FF are made using ¾"-thick veneer plywood. All the panel edges have wood veneer tape applied, and the front face has decorative moulding JJ that's 1" in from each edge. This thin decorative moulding adds visual interest to the plain, flat panel, but still lets you build a reasonably priced door. The moulding is glued and nailed in place, and all corners are mitered.

28 Drill two 35mm-diameter hinge holes on the back face of each door, 4" on center from each end. The holes are ⅛" back from the edge of the door. Clamp a straight-edged board in place to align the doors ¾" below the top edge of the lower rail. Secure the hinges in the drilled holes on each door and attach the mounting plates to the hinges. Hold the door in its normally open position and drive ⅝" wood screws through the hinge plate holes and into the stile edges to install the door.

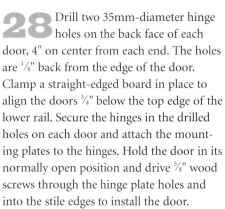

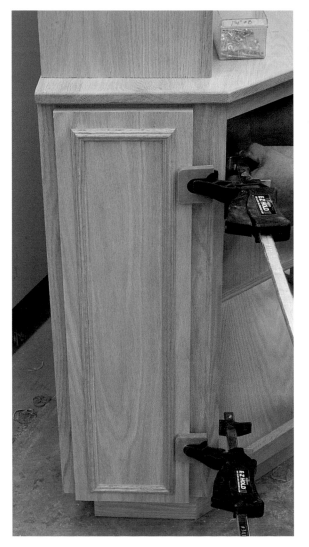

30 Attach the two 8"-wide end panels FF to the base using 1¼"-long wood screws. The screws are driven through the rear face of the rails and into the back of each panel. All doors and these end panels are aligned flush with the bottom end of the lower cabinet rails.

31 Install the two side doors EE and center door CC, using standard 100°–120° hidden hinges and face-frame mounting plates.

32 Attach the drawer face DD with two 1"-long wood screws driven through the front board of the drawer box and into the back of the drawer face. There should be a ¹⁄₂" space between the top of the center door and bottom edge of the drawer face. The easiest way to accurately locate the drawer face is to drill the handle holes only in the face. Then, align the door and drive screws through the handle holes and into the drawer box to temporarily secure the face. Gently open the drawer and install two 1¹⁄₄"-long wood screws through the drawer box. Remove the screw from the handle hole, complete the drilling, then install your handle hardware after the cabinet has been finished.

construction NOTES

Attach the top trim moulding BB, order the door and tempered shelf glass and apply the finish. Your tempered center panel door glass may be slightly different in size from mine, as it depends on the width of cut from your rabbeting bit.

Panels FF are fixed in place on my cabinet, but they can be mounted on hinges if you have easy access to both ends. You might also want to add a pullout shelf on full-extension drawer glides behind the center door for easier access to goods stored in the cabinet.

I mentioned some of the suggestions about different uses for this cabinet in the introduction. They were all valid and I'm sure there are many more applications for this versatile storage center. Don't feel restricted, however, by the sizes I used for this project. The base and hutch can be any size, and the calculations are reasonably straightforward. The base center frame can be any width. For example, if I wanted a 60"-wide base, I would increase the width of the center frame by 21", and the template would follow the new frame assembly width. The hutch backboard, top and bottom fixed shelves, rail and so on, would all have to be wider. Simply put, you can customize the cabinet size to fit your requirements.

I used flat panel doors with a little moulding, but any door style that suits your décor is fine. Once again, I built the cabinet using red oak, but you can use any wood you prefer. As I continue to say, my dimensions and designs are only suggestions, so I urge you to experiment with materials and sizes if your requirements are different from mine.

notes

coffee AND end tables

POCKET HOLE JOINERY IS AN IDEAL application to use when building tables. The skirt-to-leg joint is often made using a mortise-and-tenon joint, but screws in pocket holes, with glue, are another method. The pocket hole system can also be used to secure the tabletops.

This project is another one that deals with the construction process and not necessarily the sizes as detailed. Use the same steps to build a long and low coffee table, or a larger table that can be used as a desk. The variables are the leg lengths and tabletop dimensions.

Coffee and end tables become more than just a place to rest cups and glasses with the addition of a drawer. In television or family rooms there's often one or two remote controls, the *TV Guide*, drink coasters and other small articles that tend to clutter the tabletop surface. The small drawer that's detailed is a great place to store all those items.

End tables normally have the drawer in the end skirt, while long coffee or sofa tables have two drawers in the side skirt. These drawers are simple boxes made with Baltic birch plywood that run on wood cleats. They are simple to build and really add to the usefulness of this piece of furniture.

I built a couple of prototypes before deciding on the final size for my end table. I used some shop scraps to build the models so I could see the finished size in place. My final end table shown here is the perfect size for my sofa, and should be suitable for most applications. A coffee table to match would be lower by about 6" and almost twice as long, at about 48". Your requirements may be slightly different, but end tables that are 19" wide by 26" deep and 22" high, with a matching coffee table at 19" wide by 48" long and 16" high, should suit most rooms.

There are a few material and construction options, which I will discuss in the Construction Notes. However, these tables are always a welcome addition to any room in the home, and you'll likely build more than one set when friends and family see the finished project.

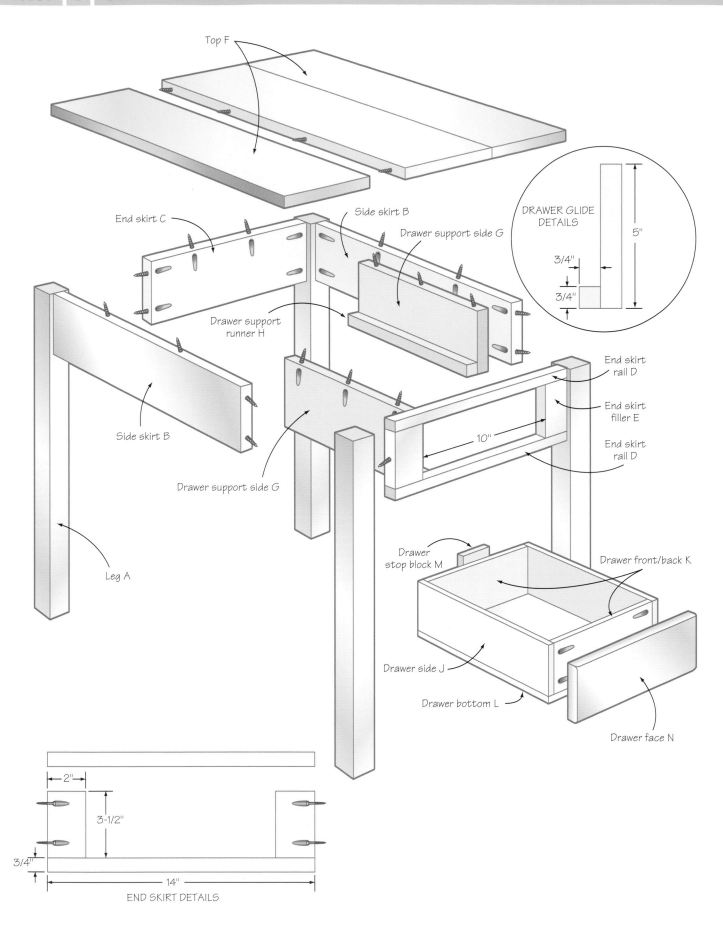

Top F

End skirt C

Side skirt B

Drawer support side G

DRAWER GLIDE
DETAILS

5"

3/4"

3/4"

Drawer support
runner H

End skirt
rail D

End skirt
filler E

Side skirt B

End skirt
rail D

10"

Drawer support side G

Leg A

Drawer
stop block M

Drawer front/back K

Drawer side J

Drawer bottom L

Drawer face N

2"

3-1/2"

3/4"

14"

END SKIRT DETAILS

inches (millimeters)

REFERENCE	QUANTITY	PART	STOCK	THICKNESS	(mm)	WIDTH	(mm)	LENGTH	(mm)	COMMENTS
A	4	legs	solid wood	$1^5/_8$	(41)	$1^5/_8$	(41)	21	(533)	
B	2	side skirts	solid wood	$3/_4$	(19)	5	(127)	21	(533)	
C	1	end skirt	solid wood	$3/_4$	(19)	5	(127)	14	(356)	
D	2	end skirt rails	solid wood	$3/_4$	(19)	$3/_4$	(19)	14	(356)	
E	2	end skirt fillers	solid wood	$3/_4$	(19)	2	(51)	$3^1/_2$	(89)	
F	1	top	solid wood	$3/_4$	(19)	$19^1/_4$	(489)	$26^1/_4$	(666)	
G	2	drawer support sides	veneer ply	$3/_4$	(19)	5	(127)	12	(305)	
H	2	drawer support runners	solid wood	$3/_4$	(19)	$3/_4$	(19)	12	(305)	
J	2	drawer sides	Baltic birch	$1/_2$	(13)	$2^7/_8$	(73)	12	(305)	
K	2	drawer back and front	Baltic birch	$1/_2$	(13)	$2^7/_8$	(73)	$8^7/_8$	(225)	
L	1	drawer bottom	Baltic birch	$1/_2$	(13)	$9^7/_8$	(251)	12	(305)	
M	1	drawer stop block	Baltic birch	$1/_2$	(13)	2	(51)	2	(51)	
N	1	drawer face	solid wood	$3/_4$	(19)	$4^1/_2$	(115)	11	(279)	

hardware AND supplies

Pocket hole screws: $1^1/_4$" (32mm), 1" (25mm)

Wood screws: 1" (25mm)

Brad nails

Glue

Drawer pull/knob

1 Cut the four legs A to the dimensions indicated in the materials list. Use a $3/_8$"-radius roundover bit to ease the four corners on each leg. The legs are standard 2×2 stock that is normally dressed to $1^5/_8$" by $1^5/_8$" and is available in most lumberyards.

2 Prepare the two sides B and one end skirt C by cutting to size and sanding. The drawer skirt board is made with parts D and E. Assemble as shown in the drawing, using glue and clamps until the adhesive sets. There should be a drawer opening that's 3½" high by 10" wide.

3 Drill pocket holes in each skirt board. Two holes are drilled on each end to attach the boards to the legs. Holes are also required to attach the tabletop, so I drilled two in the long skirt boards and two in the short boards.

4 The skirt boards are attached to the legs using 1¼" pocket hole screws and glue. If you are building softwood tables, use pocket screws. I have offset the skirt boards by ⅜" behind the face of each leg. Align the top edges of the skirt boards flush with the top ends of each leg. A simple jig with a ⅜"-deep rabbet, as shown in chapter two, is used to equally offset each skirt. The jig can be made on your table saw. A deeper rabbet will set the skirt boards farther back from the leg face, and a shallower groove will move the skirts forward.

5 The top F is made by gluing up solid-wood boards that are edge joined, glued and secured with 1¼" pocket hole screws. You can dress the edges of each board with a jointer or long-bed hand plane. However, if you don't have access to these tools, you can cut joinable edges on a table saw. To get perfect cuts, be sure the table saw blade is sharp and the fence is accurately aligned to the blade. Cut one edge, then reverse the board, with the first cut edge against the saw fence, and proceed to rip the opposite edge. If the saw is properly aligned, the edges will be parallel to each other and square. Butt the boards together and check the joints. Once the boards butt tightly, drill pocket holes and apply glue to each joined edge. Clamp the top and drive pocket hole screws into the holes to secure the panel. Set aside until the glue sets.

6 Sand the tabletop smooth, then round over the top and bottom face edges with a ⅜"-radius roundover bit. Before attaching the top, drill the center of each pocket hole with a bit that has a larger diameter than the screw. This larger hole will allow the solid-wood top to move slightly with humidity changes.

7 Center the table frame on the top with an equal overhang on all legs. Use 1¼" pocket hole screws to attach the top to the frame. Don't use any glue on this joint, so the wood will be free to move if necessary.

8 Build the two drawer supports with parts G and H. They are secured to the underside of the tabletop with 1¼" pocket hole screws. Align them so the ¾" by ¾" drawer support runners are flush with the lower skirt rail D. Remember, you can use any scrap material in your shop to build these drawer supports, because they won't be seen.

10 Install the bottom L to the box frame, using glue and brad nails.

9 The drawer box tray is made with ½"-thick Baltic birch plywood. It's a very stable sheet material that's commonly used for drawer making. The box is ⅛" narrower and ⅛" lower than the drawer box opening. Cut the parts J, K and L, then secure the back and front boards K to the sides J. The front and back should have two pocket holes drilled on each end, and are attached to the sides with 1"-long pocket hole screws and glue. Remember to set your pocket hole jig drill bit for ½"-thick material.

11 Install the drawer stop block M on the back of the drawer box. Use glue and brad nails to attach the block, positioning it ½" above the drawer box. This block will prevent the drawer from being pulled all the way out of the drawer opening.

12 The drawer face N is a piece of solid wood with the front face edges rounded over using a ⅜"-radius router bit. Center the drawer face on the box and attach it with 1"-long wood screws through the back face of the drawer box front board. The table is complete and ready for finishing. I used three coats of satin polyurethane on my table.

In the introduction to this chapter I discussed the many options available when using these construction steps for various-size tables. A coffee table that's longer and lower is an obvious companion piece to the end table, but a number of other furniture pieces can be built with these techniques. A few to consider might be a bedside table, a small utility side table for the kitchen, a tall narrow table that's typically placed behind a sofa, a writing table or a child's desk. The variations are endless because the leg and skirt construction style is used to build many different pieces of furniture.

I used oak hardwood, but any type of wood can be used. The 5"-high skirt board is a well-proportioned size for these tables, but a 6" board can also be used if you need a deeper drawer box. Thinner legs will make the table appear lighter, and can be used to match your home furnishings. A thicker 1" or 1¼" top dramatically changes the look of these tables, and would be suitable with country-style furniture.

Always secure both pieces tightly before joining, to prevent stripping the screws. Use good-quality glue and the proper screw length for each joint. Use caution when driving the screws, because a stripped thread won't provide a great deal of holding power. And with this project in particular, be sure to correctly align the top edges of the skirt boards with the top of the legs.

sofa OR hall table

THE DESIGN FOR THIS TABLE CAME from fellow woodworker Michael Brazeau of Milton, Ontario. He built a beautiful Shaker hall table with inset-style drawers and lovely tapered legs. I asked Michael if I could use his design for my book, and he agreed.

I've changed a few things in Michael's design, but retained his original concept. I decided to use overlay drawer faces and altered his drawer box guide system slightly. My table legs are also tapered, which adds greatly to the beauty of this design.

This project is called a sofa or hall table because it's equally useful behind a sofa in an area where the sofa isn't placed against a wall. If you have room in your entrance hall or foyer, this table will certainly impress your visitors. Hang a mirror over the table in your entrance way and you'll have a useful spot to rest your shopping bags or leave messages for family members.

The leg tapers appear complicated, but they are surprisingly simple to cut. There are many low-cost tapering jigs on the market, and the process is nothing more than a variation of straight cutting on the table saw. The top is detailed with a cove cut on the bottom, which lightens the overall appearance of the table. And like all the projects in this book, pocket hole joinery is the primary construction method used.

I know you'll enjoy building this table. It appears to be a complicated design with coved top and tapered legs, when, in reality, it's simple to build. This project will draw a lot of comments because the two tapered profiles on each leg create a powerful visual statement.

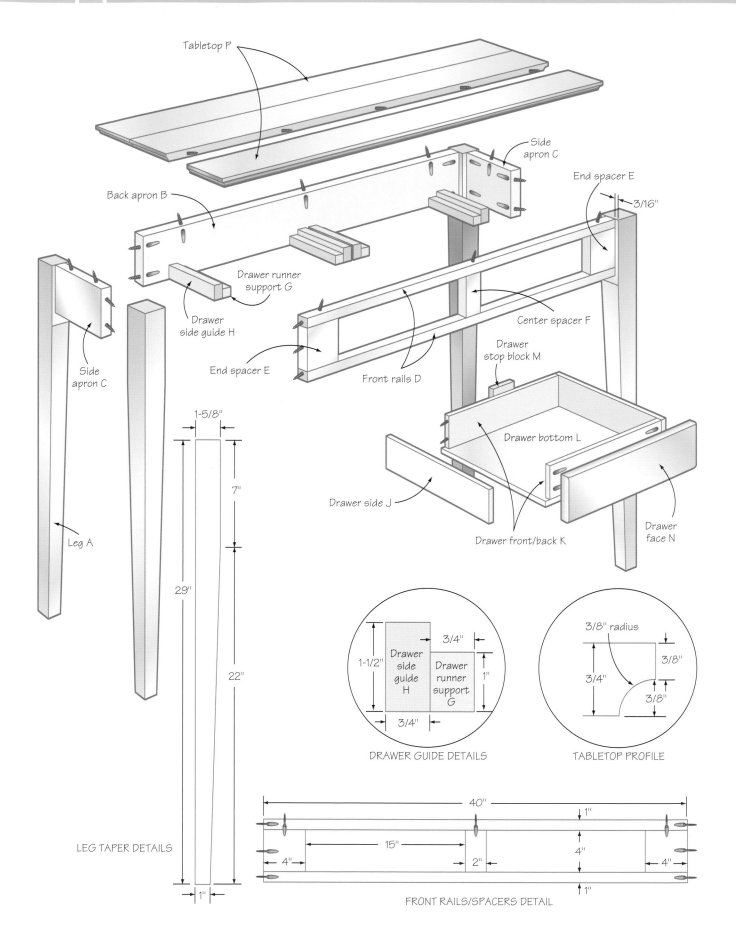

Tabletop P

Side apron C

Back apron B

End spacer E

3/16"

Drawer runner support G

Drawer side guide H

Side apron C

End spacer E

Center spacer F

Drawer stop block M

Front rails D

Drawer bottom L

Leg A

Drawer side J

Drawer front/back K

Drawer face N

1-5/8"

7"

29"

22"

1"

LEG TAPER DETAILS

DRAWER GUIDE DETAILS

Drawer side guide H

3/4"

Drawer runner support G

1-1/2"

1"

3/4"

3/8" radius

3/4"

3/8"

3/8"

TABLETOP PROFILE

40"

1"

15"

4"

4"

2"

1"

4"

FRONT RAILS/SPACERS DETAIL

inches (millimeters)

REFERENCE	QUANTITY	PART	STOCK	THICKNESS	(mm)	WIDTH	(mm)	LENGTH	(mm)	COMMENTS
A	4	legs	hardwood	$1^5/_8$	(41)	$1^5/_8$	(41)	29	(737)	taper
B	1	back apron	hardwood	$3/_4$	(19)	6	(152)	40	(1016)	
C	2	side aprons	hardwood	$3/_4$	(19)	6	(152)	7	(178)	
D	2	front rails	hardwood	$3/_4$	(19)	1	(25)	40	(1016)	
E	2	end spacers	hardwood	$3/_4$	(19)	4	(102)	4	(102)	
F	1	center spacer	hardwood	$3/_4$	(19)	2	(51)	4	(102)	
G	4	drawer runner supports	hardwood	$3/_4$	(19)	1	(25)	$7^7/_8$	(200)	
H	4	drawer side guides	hardwood	$3/_4$	(19)	$1^1/_2$	(38)	$7^7/_8$	(200)	
J	4	drawer sides	Baltic birch	$1/_2$	(13)	3	(76)	8	(203)	
K	4	drawer backs and fronts	Baltic birch	$1/_2$	(13)	3	(76)	$13^7/_8$	(352)	
L	2	drawer bottoms	Baltic birch	$1/_2$	(13)	8	(203)	$14^7/_8$	(378)	
M	2	drawer stops	Baltic birch	$1/_2$	(13)	3	(76)	2	(51)	
N	2	drawer faces	hardwood	$3/_4$	(19)	5	(127)	16	(406)	
P	1	tabletop	hardwood	$3/_4$	(19)	$12^1/_2$	(318)	$47^1/_4$	(1200)	

hardware AND supplies

Pocket hole screws: $1^1/_4$ (32mm), 1" (25mm)

Wood screws: $1^1/_2$ (38mm), 1" (25mm)

Brad nails

Glue

Drawer knobs

1 The four legs A are made using standard $1^5/_8$"-square stock, cut 29" long. The taper on two adjoining sides of each leg begins 7" from the top and tapers from $1^5/_8$" to 1" at the bottom. Mark the tapered cut sides to make assembly easier and errorproof. Tapering jigs are easy to make, and there are a number of plans in books about shop jig construction. However, a taper jig is an inexpensive tool costing about $20. Follow the details in the drawing, and make a few test-cuts with scrap lumber before beginning the final cut on each leg. Remember this important note: Two adjoining faces on each leg should be tapered. That will allow us to attach the skirt boards to the legs with tapers facing inward or toward each other.

2 The two sides C and back B aprons are solid hardwood. Cut them to the sizes indicated in the materials list, then drill two pocket holes in each end on all three boards. Before beginning the assembly steps, drill three pocket holes on the upper inside edge of the back apron and two in the side aprons. These holes will be used to secure the tabletop. Join the three aprons to the legs with glue and $1^1/_4$"-long pocket hole screws. Inset the aprons on each leg by $3/_16$". Remember, the two side tapers on each leg face inward and toward each other. Use the offset jig that was described in chapter two when attaching the aprons.

3 The four table legs should now be joined by the side and back aprons. Verify that all leg tapers face inward, toward a leg on the front and back of the table frame.

4 Prepare the front rails D and spacers E and F, as detailed in the materials list. Glue the rails to the spacers, following the drawing detail, and secure with 1½"-long wood screws to form the front apron assembly.

5 The front apron should have two pocket holes drilled on each end. As well, drill three holes along the top edge that will be used to secure the tabletop. Once the front apron drilling is finished, it can be attached to the legs with glue and 1¼" pocket hole screws. The front apron assembly should also be inset ³⁄₁₆" back from the front face of each leg.

shop TIP

Cut all the front apron assembly pieces from one board and maintain their position as parts of the whole board. By keeping them in order, the cut boards, once assembled, will appear as one board because the grain pattern was maintained.

6 Build the four drawer runner assemblies, using the runner supports G and side guides H. The assemblies are constructed using glue and brad nails. Runner assemblies are set flush with the top edge of the lower rail and front apron spacers. Drill pocket holes in the bottom edge of side guides H, and attach the assemblies with 1¼" pocket hole screws and glue.

7 The four drawer runner assemblies should be aligned as shown.

8 I am using ½"-thick Baltic birch, sometimes called cabinet-grade plywood, to build two drawer boxes. The overall size of these drawer boxes will be ⅛" narrower than the drawer openings in the front rail, and 3½" high. Cut all the drawer box parts J, K and L to the sizes indicated in the materials list. Then, drill two pocket holes on each end of the outside faces on the fronts and backs K. Remember to set your pocket hole drill-stop guide for ½"-thick material. Attach the fronts and backs to the sides with 1" pocket hole screws and glue. The bottoms L are secured with glue and brad nails.

9 Install the two drawer stops M on the backboard of each drawer box. These stops are attached with glue and brad nails, and are 1" above the top edge of the backboards. They are used to prevent the drawer from being pulled all the way out.

10 The two drawer faces N are solid wood with their front face edges rounded over using a ¼" roundover router bit. They are aligned on the box so they extend ½" beyond the drawer opening on all edges of the front apron. Use 1"-long wood screws, driven from the inside of the drawer box, to attach the faces.

11 Glue up enough boards to form the finished tabletop P, measuring 12½" deep by 47¼" long. Use 1¼" pocket hole screws and glue to join the boards.

12 Use a cove bit to profile the lower edge of the tabletop. Cut the cove just deep enough to leave a ⅜"-high straight edge on the top side. Before attaching the top, enlarge the screw shaft-hole diameter of the pocket holes to provide expansion room for the solid-wood top. The screw hole should be double the screw shaft diameter.

13 Attach the top using 1¼" pocket hole screws in the previously drilled pocket holes. There should be an overhang of 2" on each end and 1⅛" on the front and back side of the table. All overhang dimensions are measured from the leg faces to the tabletop edges. Notice that the cove cut is on the underside of the tabletop after installation.

construction NOTES

As always, please ignore the type of wood I've used, in this case red oak, because I'm making this table to match my existing furniture. Any wood species can be used, and woods like mahogany, quarter-sawn oak, maple and pine are also commonly used for this Shaker-style furniture.

The leg tapers appear difficult, but as I previously mentioned, they are simply a variation of a straight cut on the table saw. Taper jigs are inexpensive, and every woodworker should have one in their shop. I realize that I'm repeating this word of caution, but be sure the leg tapers are facing each other. Mark the taper cuts as they are done on the saw to prevent improper placement. An error at this point, after the table legs have been assembled with glue, can ruin your project.

If you don't like the tapered leg look, this sofa or hall table can be built using straight 1⅝"-square stock. The straight edges of the lumber can be rounded over with a router bit or left square. A straight leg will make the table appear more Colonial in style, particularly if the bottom cove cut on the tabletop is substituted with a roundover profile on the bottom and top faces.

My table is a specific width and height to meet my requirements. Yours can be any size and depends a great deal on where it will be used. If you plan on putting it behind a sofa, measure the height of that piece of furniture and adjust the table dimensions accordingly. A table too high or too low behind a sofa will not look right, so use some scrap materials to create a test table and view it at different levels until you find the right dimensions.

notes

framed mirror

I DESIGNED THIS FRAMED MIRROR FOR a couple of reasons. First, I needed a hall mirror for my home. Second, I was anxious to use the pocket hole filler plugs as a decorative element on a large frame, and this was the perfect project.

A wise old cabinetmaker that I knew, when speaking about joinery, said, "If you can't hide it, celebrate it." That's the case with these visible pocket holes. I could have put them on the back side of the frame but decided to show them off — and I think they look great!

This elegant mirror is simple to build and will be a useful addition for the hall, or any room in your home. It can be used in the bathroom as a vanity mirror, in a bedroom as a dresser mirror or as an accent piece in any small room that needs to look larger. A mirror always seems to enlarge a space, so it would be perfect in a small dining room.

One of the advantages of being a woodworker is the ability to custom design and build projects for a specific purpose. There are many framed mirrors available in the marketplace, but you'd have to settle for a standard size. A woodworker can build to any size, and that's a big plus with this project. It's a real bonus because buying a custom-size framed mirror would be an expensive proposition.

I used a visual trick with this project by making the top edge of the mirror appear curved. In reality, it's a straight-cut plate mirror that's much less expensive than a curved cut; only the top rail of the frame is arched. As I said, it's an easy project to build, so have fun making this popular framed mirror.

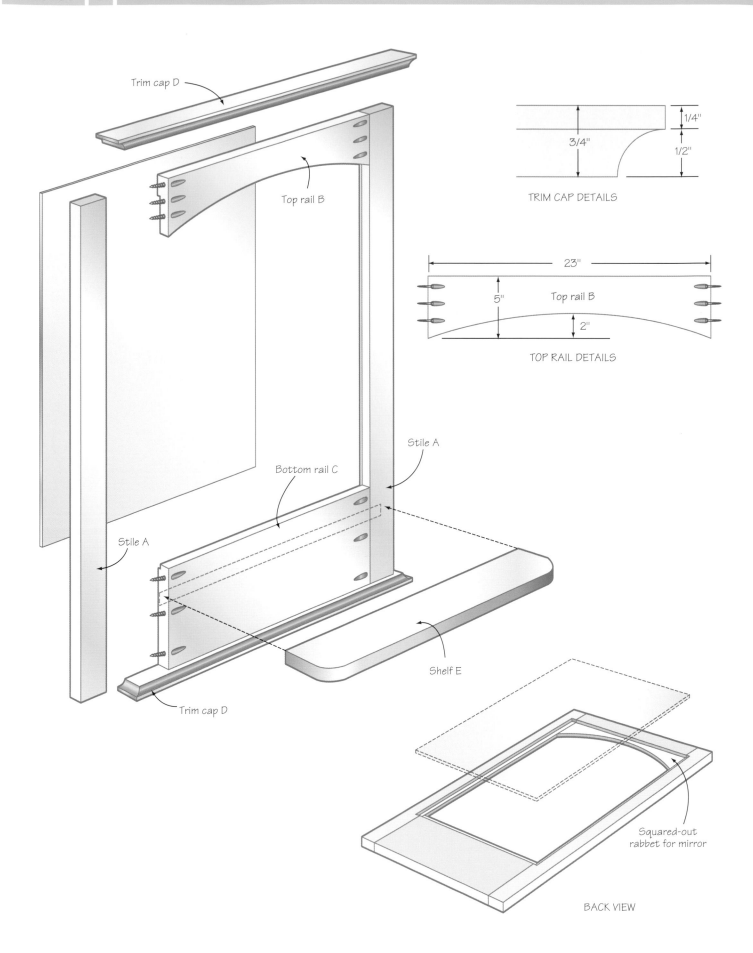

Trim cap D

Top rail B

Stile A

Bottom rail C

Stile A

Trim cap D

Shelf E

TRIM CAP DETAILS

1/4"

3/4"

1/2"

TOP RAIL DETAILS

23"

5"

Top rail B

2"

Squared-out
rabbet for mirror

BACK VIEW

inches (millimeters)

REFERENCE	QUANTITY	PART	STOCK	THICKNESS	(mm)	WIDTH	(mm)	LENGTH	(mm)	COMMENTS
A	2	stiles	hardwood	$^3/_4$	(19)	$2^1/_2$	(64)	38	(965)	
B	1	top rail	hardwood	$^3/_4$	(19)	5	(127)	23	(584)	
C	1	bottom rail	hardwood	$^3/_4$	(19)	$7^1/_4$	(184)	23	(584)	
D	2	trim caps	hardwood	$^3/_4$	(19)	$1^5/_8$	(41)	30	(762)	
E	1	shelf	hardwood	$^3/_4$	(19)	$3^1/_2$	(89)	26	(660)	
F	1	mirror plate		$^3/_{16}$	(5)					approximately $23^5/_8$" (600) × $28^7/_8$" (733); cut to the size required

hardware AND supplies

Pocket hole screws: $1^1/_4$" (32mm)

Wood screws: $1^1/_2$" (38mm), $^1/_2$" (13mm)

Glue

Pocket hole plugs

Mirror clips

Mirror hangers

1 Cut the four frame parts A, B and C, as indicated in the materials list. Draw an arc on the top rail B, following the dimensions shown in the illustration. Use a thin strip of wood, bent around finishing nails along the arc, to mark the pattern. Then, use a jigsaw or scroll saw to form the arc.

2 Drill three equally spaced pocket holes on the ends of each rail B and C. Set your drill bit stop collar so the pocket hole will be about $\frac{1}{8}$" deeper than normal. These pocket holes will be filled with wood plugs, and I want to make sure they are seated deep in the hole without being limited by the screw head.

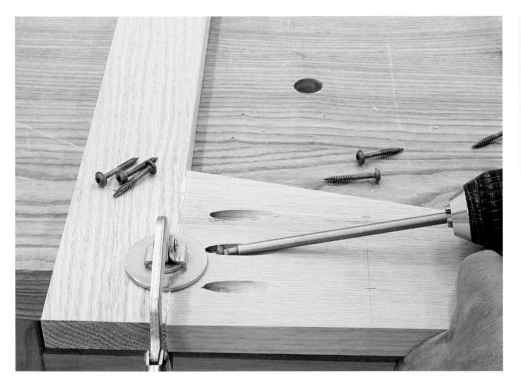

shop TIP

I'm drilling my pocket holes on the front face of the frame members. However, you may want to skip the wood plug step and hide the holes on the back side of the mirror frame. Either option is acceptable.

3 Join both rails to the stiles using glue and $1\frac{1}{4}$"-long pocket hole screws. The outside edges of the rails are set flush with the ends of each stile.

4 Fill the pocket holes with wood plugs. I am using walnut plugs on this oak frame as a decorative element; however, any combination, including plugs of the same wood species, is fine and really a matter of personal taste. Use glue in the pocket holes, insert the plugs and, when the adhesive has cured, sand the plugs flat to the frame surface.

5 Ease the inside frame profile, using a $\frac{3}{8}$"-radius router bit. Then complete the final sanding of the frame front face.

6 Use a rabbeting router bit to cut a $\frac{3}{16}$"-deep rabbet on the inside back profile of the frame. This will provide a place for the mirror plate to rest. Each rabbeting bit cuts a little differently because of the bit style and diameter of the guide bearing. The width is not critical as the mirror will be ordered to fit the cut you create.

7 You can order the mirror plate cut with a curved top but that would be expensive. I want to use a plain, square-cut mirror, so I will have to square the rabbet on the curved top rail. Use a straight-cutting bit in your router, guided by a board, to clean out most of the wood. Remove the remaining material and square the corners, using a sharp chisel.

8 The upper and lower trim caps D are formed with a cove router bit. The cove is cut leaving a $\frac{1}{4}$"-high lip on the edge. Cove cut the front edge and ends of both pieces. The cove faces the frame on both bottom and top caps, and is centered on the frame. Use glue and $1\frac{1}{2}$"-long wood screws to secure the trim caps. The back edges of D are flush with the back face of the frame.

9 Shelf E is attached with glue and $1\frac{1}{2}$"-long wood screws driven through the back face of the frame. Round over the two outside corners of this shelf to minimize injury in case someone bumps into the mirror. I set my shelf board $2\frac{1}{2}$" below the bottom rail's top edge and centered on the frame's width.

10 Use a ¼"-radius roundover bit to ease the outside edges of the frame stiles. The router base plate will strike the upper and lower trim cap, limiting its travel. However, that's the effect I want to achieve on those edges. Prior to installing the mirror, apply a finish to your frame.

11 I'm using metal clips to hold the mirror in place on the frame. The bent clips are installed in ⅛"-deep grooves that I've cut into the frame edge with a straight router bit. The clips are held in place with ½"-long wood screws. I also installed heavy-duty hanger clips on the frame for mounting on screws driven into the wall. If possible, attach the hanger clips to the stiles so the upper rail doesn't support the mirror's weight.

construction NOTES

This mirror can be any size, as previously mentioned. Different applications demand special sizing, so change the dimensions to suit your needs.

Any wood type can be used, and the pocket holes can just as easily be filled with matching or contrasting plugs. I applied three coats of polyurethane to the frame, but an applied stain, to match existing furniture color, is often necessary.

Be careful when installing the mirror clips, as too much pressure can crack the glass. You should also order the mirror ⅛" smaller than the overall width and height to accommodate any seasonal wood movement. My mirror supplier uses a standard 5mm-thick plate, and I'm sure that's a common thickness, but check with your supplier before cutting the rabbets on your frame.

The curved upper rail is a nice design element and adds a lot of interest to the mirror. However, it's not always suitable for some furniture styles. If your furniture has straight lines, as is the case for some styles like Shaker, you may want to eliminate the upper rail curve. As well, the coved caps may not suit the furniture style in your home. However, they can be almost any design, including straight line with cuts, bullnose or a simple roundover, so change them to meet your needs.

pendulum wall clock

A WALL CLOCK IS AN ENJOYABLE project project to build, and one that I like doing but never seem to have the time for — no pun intended. When I was designing the projects for this book, I realized that pocket hole joinery could be used to make the clock, as well as adding a unique decorative element. The finished project is beautiful, and the wood-filled pocket holes are drawing a lot of positive comments.

I used my favorite hardwood and installed contrasting wood plugs. The red oak with walnut plugs is a nice combination of woods, and the appearance isn't overpowering. In some furniture designs, the decorative trim is so obvious that it becomes the focus. These two woods, after being finished with spray lacquer, are a nice gold and brown mixture.

A wall clock would be a great addition to any room in your house. It's functional and isn't all that expensive to build. The hardware, including the glass, totals less than $35. A single AA battery powers the quartz clock and pendulum mechanism.

This wall clock is unique and would be a nice gift for someone on that special occasion. It's something that will be used every day and will be passed down to future generations. I've had three or four family members remark, "Oh, that's nice. Can you make me one?" So, be sure to note all the measurements and construction steps, because you, too, will be building a few more clocks.

Purchase a clock kit that allows you to change the pendulum length to suit your cabinet size. My kit doesn't have chimes, but I did notice two or three slightly higher priced kits that were equipped with that feature. Some people, myself included, don't appreciate the chimes sounding every hour, but many like the sound, so the choice is yours.

Take your time building the wall clock, and try a few different trim combinations. This is one project you'll be looking at for many years, so be sure you're satisfied with the results. And if you sell woodcrafts, this clock would be a big seller at any show.

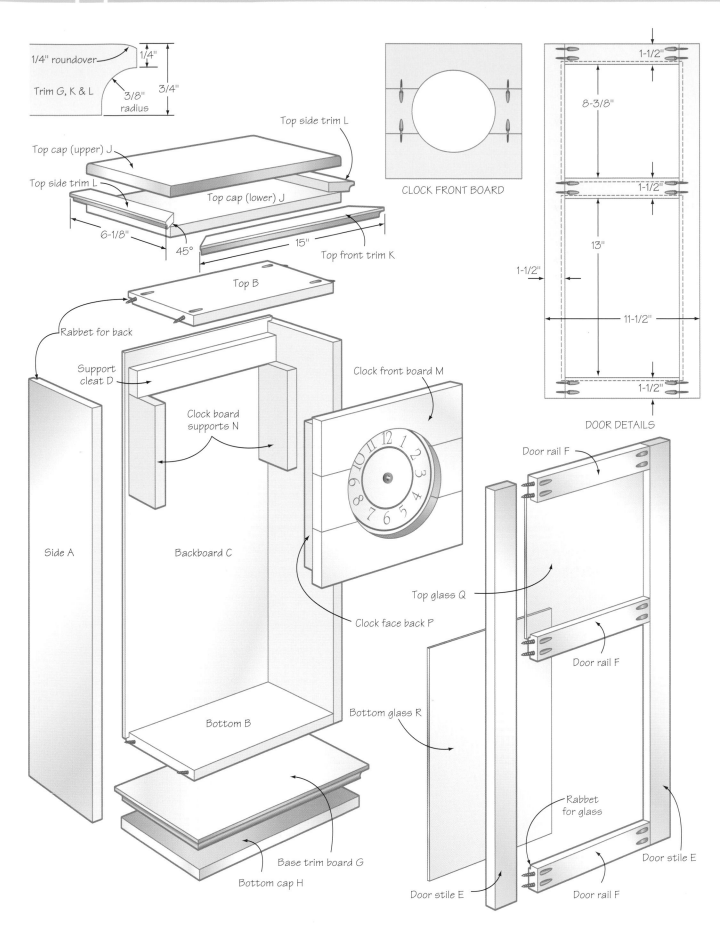

1/4" roundover

1/4"

Trim G, K & L

3/8" radius

3/4"

Top side trim L

Top cap (upper) J

Top side trim L

Top cap (lower) J

6-1/8"

45°

15"

Top front trim K

CLOCK FRONT BOARD

1-1/2"

8-3/8"

1-1/2"

13"

1-1/2"

11-1/2"

1-1/2"

DOOR DETAILS

Top B

Rabbet for back

Support cleat D

Clock board supports N

Clock front board M

Side A

Backboard C

Clock face back P

Top glass Q

Door rail F

Door rail F

Bottom B

Bottom glass R

Rabbet for glass

Base trim board G

Bottom cap H

Door stile E

Door rail F

Door stile E

inches (millimeters)

REFERENCE	QUANTITY	PART	STOCK	THICKNESS	(mm)	WIDTH	(mm)	LENGTH	(mm)	COMMENTS
A	2	sides	hardwood	³/₄	(19)	4¹/₂	(115)	26	(660)	
B	2	top and bottom	hardwood	³/₄	(19)	4¹/₂	(115)	10	(254)	
C	1	backboard	veneer ply	¹/₄	(6)	10³/₄	(273)	25¹/₄	(641)	
D	1	support cleat	hardwood	³/₄	(19)	1¹/₂	(38)	10	(254)	
E	2	door stiles	hardwood	³/₄	(19)	1¹/₂	(38)	25⁷/₈	(657)	
F	3	door rails	hardwood	³/₄	(19)	1¹/₂	(38)	8¹/₂	(216)	
G	1	base trim board	hardwood	³/₄	(19)	5¹/₄	(133)	13	(330)	
H	1	bottom cap	hardwood	³/₄	(19)	4³/₄	(121)	12¹/₁₆	(307)	
J	2	top caps	hardwood	³/₄	(19)	5¹/₄	(133)	13	(330)	
K	1	top front trim	hardwood	³/₄	(19)	1¹/₂	(38)	15	(381)	
L	2	top side trim	hardwood	³/₄	(19)	1¹/₂	(38)	6¹/₈	(155)	
M	1	clock front board	hardwood	³/₄	(19)	9¹⁵/₁₆	(253)	9¹⁵/₁₆	(253)	
N	2	clock board supports	hardwood	³/₄	(19)	2¹/₂	(64)	6	(152)	
P	1	clock face back	particleboard	⁵/₈	(16)	7¹/₂	(191)	7¹/₂	(191)	
Q	1	top glass	glass	¹/₈	(3)	9¹/₄	(235)	9¹/₈	(232)	
R	1	bottom glass	glass	¹/₈	(3)	9¹/₄	(235)	13⁵/₈	(346)	

hardware AND supplies

	Pocket hole screws: 1¹/₄" (32mm)
	Wood screws: 1¹/₄" (32mm), 1" (25mm)
	1¹/₄" (32mm) decorative wood screws
	Brad nails
	Glue
	Pocket hole plugs
1	Clock face kit item #46K05.17 Lee Valley
1	Clock mechanism item #46K01.09 Lee Valley
2	No-mortise hinges
	Glass retainer clips
	Door latch

1 Purchase your clock and pendulum kit prior to finalizing the cabinet dimensions to ensure a proper fit. My clock face is 6" in diameter, painted on a 7½" square plate. These kits are popular and available at many woodworking hardware supply stores.

2 Cut the two sides A, as well as the top and bottom B, to the sizes shown in the materials list. Form a rabbet with your table saw, ¼" deep by ⅜" wide, on the rear inside face of each board. These rabbets can be cut along the full length of each board, because they will be covered by other trim pieces.

3 Drill pocket holes on both side edges of the top and bottom boards. Secure them to the clock sides using glue and 1¼"-long pocket hole screws.

shop TIP

There has to be enough room to properly install wood filler plugs in the holes. I experimented with a couple of pocket hole drill setups, and found that setting my stop collar on the drill bit to drill a deeper hole worked best. I set the stop about ⅛" deeper than my standard ¾" material setting. The large heads of the pocket hole screws could then be driven a little deeper in the hole, providing more room to seat the wood plugs.

4 The backboard C is attached to the clock cabinet with brad nails and glue. The backboard should sit in the rabbets on all four panels.

5 Install the support cleat D, using glue and 1¼" wood screws through the top board. A hole can be drilled in the center of this cleat, through the backboard, which can be used to hang the clock. I will be putting a 3" screw into a wall stud to mount the clock.

6 The door is 25⅞" high by 11½" wide. The two stiles E (vertical members) and the three rails F (horizontal members) are 1½" wide. The rails are joined to the stiles with two 1¼" pocket hole screws and glue at each joint. I used walnut plugs to contrast with the oak door-frame, in the pocket holes on the front face of the doorframe. Carefully align and drill the pocket holes if they are to be on the front face of the door. If you prefer, the pocket holes, filled with matching wood plugs, can be on the back face of the door. Position the rails and stiles as shown in the illustration.

7 Use glue to install the wood pocket hole plugs, and sand them smooth once the adhesive has set.

8 Cut a recess on the back of both frame openings, using a rabbeting router bit. The rabbet should be ³⁄₁₆" deep to hold the glass panels. The rabbet width is dependent on your router bit, but should be at least ¼" wide. Square the corners with a chisel.

9 Complete the machine work on the door by rounding over the outside profile with a $\frac{1}{4}$"-radius router bit.

10 The first trim board is attached to the bottom of the wall clock cabinet. Cut base trim board G to the size indicated in the materials list. Use a $\frac{3}{8}$"-radius cove router bit to cut a profile on the bottom edge of the front and sides of this trim board. The top face of the board's front and side edges are rounded over with a $\frac{1}{4}$"-radius router bit. Trim board G overhangs each side, as well as the front edge of the cabinet, by $\frac{3}{4}$". Attach this trim board to the bottom of the clock cabinet with glue and $1\frac{1}{4}$" wood screws.

11 The bottom cap H has the front and side edges of its lower face rounded over with a $\frac{1}{4}$"-radius bit. All the edges on this trim board should align with the edges of the coved trim board G. Note that the dimensions of your bottom cap may be slightly different from mine because of the profile on the cove bit you own. Verify the exact dimensions of cap board H before cutting to size. Use glue and clamps to secure the bottom cap H to the underside of G. Once the adhesive has set, sand the G-to-H edges smooth.

12 The lower top cap J is installed with glue and 1¼"-long wood screws. Round over the bottom face edges on the sides and front with a ¼" router bit. This cap overhangs the sides and front edge by ¾". Use a cove bit to profile the lower edges of the three top trim boards K and L. Attach them to the lower top cap with glue and brad nails. The cove cuts on these three boards face toward the clock. There should be a ¼" straight lip on each board after completing the cove profiles. Align the trim boards so their back edges are ½" in from the front edge of the lower cap J. Join the two corners with 45° miter cuts.

13 Attach the upper top cap J. The top face edges are rounded over with a ¼"-radius bit. This cap is aligned with the lower top cap and secured with glue and brad nails.

14 Glue up enough boards to achieve the final size for the clock front board M, as detailed in the materials list. You can use a single board if you have one that's large enough, or join a number of narrower boards. If you are joining boards, carefully position the pocket holes to leave room for a 6⅛"-diameter hole in the center.

15 Cut the 6⅛"-diameter hole in M, or to a size that's suitable for your clock face, in the center of this panel. Use a jigsaw or scroll saw to cut the hole and sand smooth after completing the cut. Profile the front edge of the hole with a ¼"-radius router bit.

16 Cut and install the two clock board supports N with glue and brad nails. These two boards will support the clock face board and position it 1" below the front edges of the cabinet sides. That 1" inset will leave enough clearance for the door hinges.

17 The clock face is attached to the support boards with 1¼" decorative wood screws. They can be easily removed when the clock battery needs replacing. One on each side, threaded into the supports N, will secure the face.

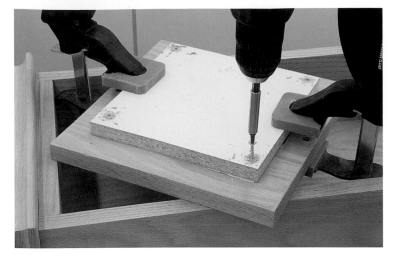

18 My clock face is 6" in diameter, painted on a 7½"-square sheet of thin metal. The clock motor assembly I purchased is designed for mounting on a ⅝"-thick piece of material. I used double-stick tape to attach the clock face to a ⅝"-thick sheet of melamine particleboard (PB). Once the clock face is attached to the clock face back P, center the assembly in the hole on the clock front board M. Use four 1"-long wood screws to join the boards.

19 Drill a hole for the clock motor shaft and test fit the mechanism. When you're satisfied that the clock assembly is working correctly, remove the hardware and apply a finish to the wood. I used three coats of polyurethane, sanding with 220-grit paper between coats.

20 Dozens of hinge styles can be used to hang the cabinet door. I used no-mortise hardware mounted 4" on center from the top and bottom to install my door.

21 The two glass panels Q and R are secured with small plastic clips that are readily available in hardware stores. Be sure to position the clips so they won't hit the cabinet side boards.

22 I installed a spring latch to hold the wall clock door closed. However, a number of other latches are available, including the common magnetic type. Use whichever style of latch hardware you prefer.

construction NOTES

I always remind woodworkers about using their favorite wood species, and this project is no different. I used red oak because it's reasonably priced in my area, and I like working with that type of wood. However, this wall clock can be built with any type of wood, and the choice is often dictated by existing room furniture. The project would be very striking if it were made of walnut with visible oak pocket hole plugs.

The size of this clock was based on the dimensions of my hardware. That's the reason I suggest you purchase your clock kit before cutting any wood. I looked through a few woodworking catalogs and found kits with similar dimensions, so I'm sure it won't be too difficult to get one that's sized close to the one I used.

One of the main design features of this project was the use of filled pocket holes on the front face of the clock cabinet door. It's an interesting effect and has drawn a lot of positive comments. However, you can just as easily drill the pocket holes on the back face of the door.

The cabinet box is simple and consists of two sides, a bottom and top, with a ¼" backboard. The upper and lower trim details define the style, and it's here where you can create your own special look. Experiment with different store-bought and shop-made mouldings until you find a combination that suits your furniture style.

I considered putting hinges on the clock front board, but decided that a battery change every six or eight months wasn't enough to justify the added hardware cost. As it turns out, I found I could change the battery by reaching behind the clock board, so I didn't have to remove it. However, I would still recommend using the removable decorative screws in case the mechanism requires replacement.

The building steps for this wall clock can be used to build a floor model, if desired. I'd suggest a larger clock face, a longer pendulum and some minor design changes on the base. The clock case can be smaller or larger, with a few minor dimensional changes, so it's a versatile project.

I also thought about purchasing a better mechanism, possibly a plug-in powered model, and installing a light behind the clock face board to illuminate the case. It would be a dramatic effect, and one that might be worth researching. Clocks are fun to build and will usually remain in the family for years, so it's well worth trying a few design ideas until you get one that's right for you.

notes

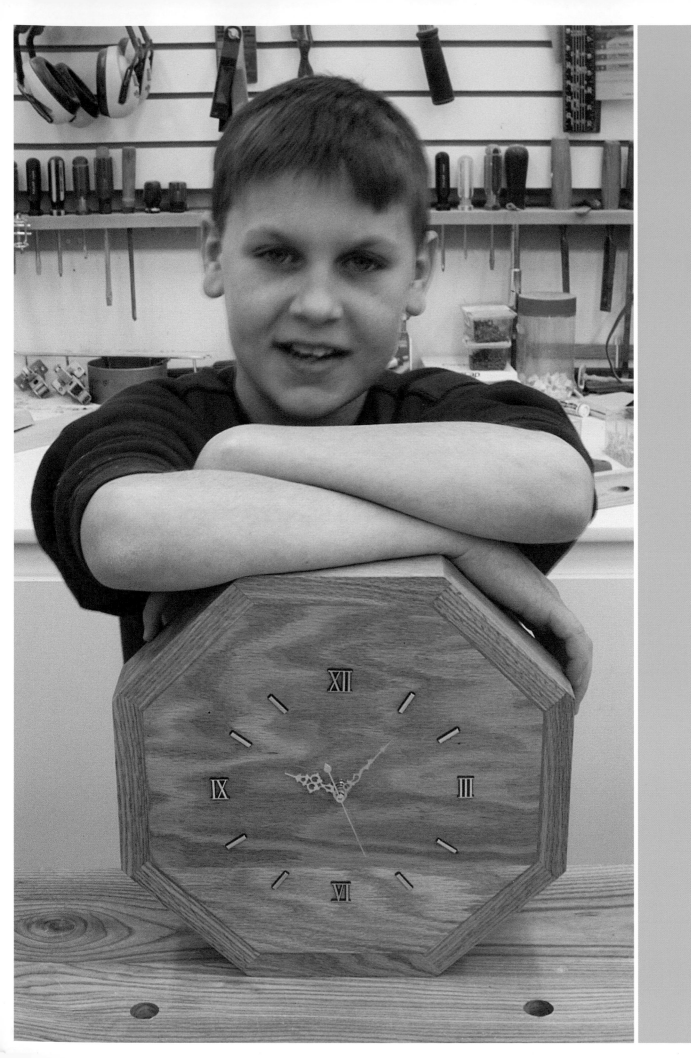

child's wall clock

THIS PROJECT IS PERFECT FOR THOSE of you who have youngsters interested in woodworking. It provides quick rewards because they have a finished project in about two hours, and it's a unique piece that they can show to their friends. More importantly, the project can be used as a fun learning tool to teach them about geometry and time. The clock has a diameter of about 11½" and can be easily hung on the wall.

My nephew Cody was over for his Saturday woodworking session and was willing to tackle any project I had in mind. I always try to pick projects that have educational value. I don't want the children to simply go away with a few sticks they put together; I want them to learn something of value. You normally have their undivided attention, so it's an ideal opportunity to teach in a fun environment.

This project involves geometry and the relationship of a multisided figure that returns to its start point. What are the angles at each intersection of a hexagon or octa-

gon? These geometrical figures form a circle which has 360°. To find the angle on intersection where each board meets, you must divide the number of sides into the total degrees of a circle. In this case, an eight-sided octagon, divided into 360°, means each angle must be 45° (360/8 = 45). In traditional woodworking joinery, each piece of the joint would be 22½° to form a 45° intersection, but pocket hole joinery is a little different.

In chapter two, I detailed face-angle joinery, and the jig that is used to join wood at an angle using pocket hole screws. The eight sides of this octagon are joined in that manner, using the 45° jig to support the wood.

This project is the perfect teaching tool, which will capture your child's attention for two hours. The final result is a completed project that's unique and ready to hang on a wall in their room. Having fun, learning and getting quick results with a finished project — what more could a child (or an adult, for that matter) want!

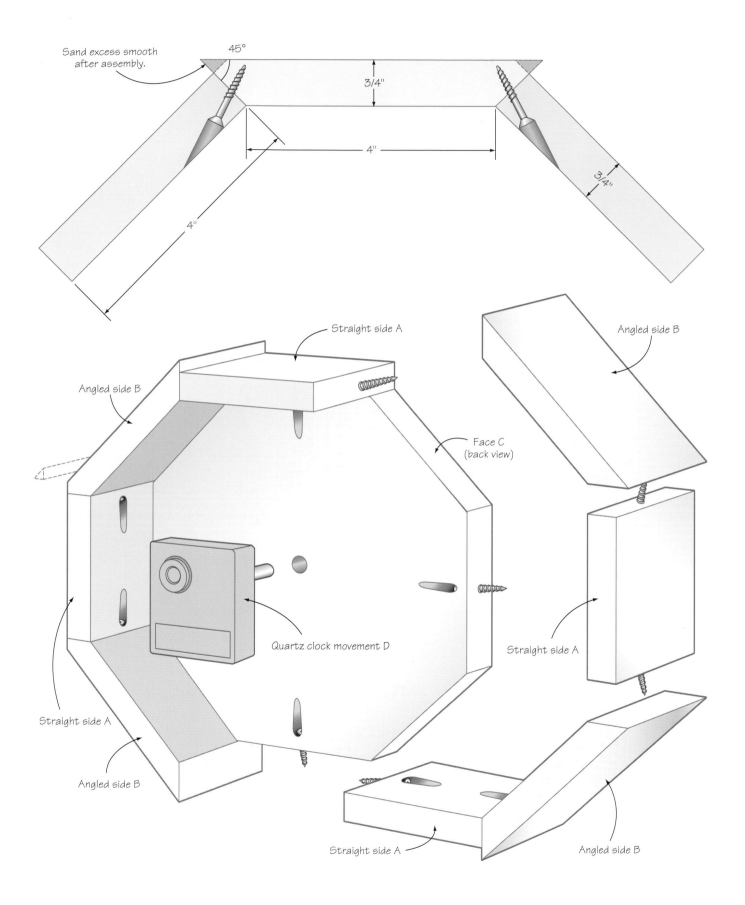

Sand excess smooth after assembly.

45°

3/4"

4"

3/4"

4"

Straight side A

Angled side B

Angled side B

Face C (back view)

Straight side A

Quartz clock movement D

Straight side A

Straight side A

Angled side B

Straight side A

Angled side B

inches (millimeters)

REFERENCE	QUANTITY	PART	STOCK	THICKNESS	(mm)	WIDTH	(mm)	LENGTH	(mm)	COMMENTS
A	4	straight sides	solid wood	3/4	(19)	2	(51)	4	(102)	
B	4	angled sides	solid wood	3/4	(19)	2	(51)	4	(102)	
C	1	face	veneer PB	11/16	(18)	11	(279)	11	(279)	cut as detailed
D	1	quartz clock movement								

Note: PB = particleboard.

hardware AND supplies

Pocket hole screws, 1¼" (32mm), 1" (25mm)

Glue

1 Cut the eight clock ring pieces A and B. The straight sides are 4" long and cut at 90°. The four angled pieces have a 45° miter on each end and are 4" long, measured at the shortest (inside) cuts of the miter. Test fit all the parts, alternating the straight and angled boards, before beginning the assembly.

2 Drill a pocket hole on each end of the straight sides A.

3 Build a 45° angled-support jig and join the straight boards, to the angled boards using glue and 1¼" pocket hole screws. The inside faces of all the pieces must be aligned. The space becomes restricted as the assembly progresses, so a screwdriver bit in a small ratchet can be used to drive the pocket hole screws. Clamp both pieces of the joint to prevent movement as you're driving the screws.

4 A part of each angled piece will be outside the clock ring, which is normal when joining angled parts with pocket holes. Remove the excess wood using a belt or disc sander.

5 Put the assembly on a piece of ⅝"- or ¹¹⁄₁₆"-thick veneer particleboard and mark the inside profile of the clock ring. Use a miter saw, band saw or scroll saw to cut the face. If you haven't got a power miter saw, the face can be cut with a handsaw and a straightedge to guide the blade.

6 Drill four pocket holes on the back side of the clock face. Attach the face to the clock ring with 1" pocket hole screws, being sure to clamp both securely, so the front of the face is flush with the front edge of the clock ring.

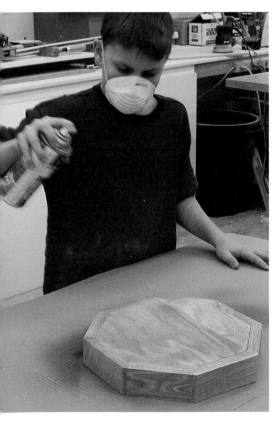

7 Apply the finish before installing the clock mechanism. Cody used three coats of fast-drying spray lacquer.

8 I purchased an inexpensive quartz clock kit that is powered by a single AA battery. The kit came with installation instructions for hole requirements, and a set of self-adhesive numbers for the clock face.

construction
NOTES

I haven't built many clocks or purchased kits, so I was amazed at how popular this hobby has become and the variety of hardware that's available. I would suggest buying the clock mechanism before you start, in case you want to change the face size to match the hardware.

Making each ring piece shorter or longer can change the size of the face. If you want a different size, create a scale drawing of the clock ring. Small dimensional changes either way will alter the final size dramatically.

I first experimented with 1½"-wide boards for the clock ring, but found it wasn't deep enough for the clock hardware I used. Once again, I suggest purchasing the hardware before cutting, to be sure the interior depth is suitable.

notes

suppliers

Many suppliers contributed products, material and technical support during the project building phase.

I appreciate how helpful they've been and recommend the companies without hesitation.

If you have trouble locating a product that I've mentioned, please e-mail me at danny@cabinetmaking.com.

ADAMS & KENNEDY — THE WOOD SOURCE
6178 Mitch Owen Road
P.O. Box 700
Manotick, Ontario, Canada K4M 1A6
613-822-6800
www.wood-source.com
Wood supply

ADJUSTABLE CLAMP COMPANY
417 North Ashland Avenue
Chicago, Illinois 60622
312-666-0640
www.adjustableclamp.com
Clamps

BIESEMEYER WOODWORKING TOOLS
216 South Alma School Road, Suite 3
Mesa, Arizona 85210
800-782-1831
www.biesemeyer.com
Fences, guards, splitters

CONSTANTINES WOOD CENTER
1040 East Oakland Park Boulevard
Fort Lauderdale, Florida 33334
954-561-1716
www.constantines.com
Tools, woods, veneers, hardware

DELTA MACHINERY
4825 Highway 45 North
P.O. Box 2468
Jackson, Tennessee 38302-2468
800-223-7278 (U.S.)
800-463-3582 (Canada)
www.deltawoodworking.com
Woodworking tools

EXAKTOR PRECISION WOODWORKING TOOLS, INC.
4 Glenbourne Park
Markham, Ontario, Canada L6C 1G9
800-387-9789
www.exaktortools.com
Accessories for the table saw

FORREST MANUFACTURING COMPANY, INC.
461 River Road
Clifton, New Jersey 07014
800-733-7111
forrest.woodmall.com
Carbide-tipped saw blades, dado sets, sharpening

FREUD TOOLS
218 Feld Avenue
High Point, North Carolina 27263
800-334-4107
www.freudtools.com
Carbide-tipped saw blades, dado sets, tooling

GARRETT WADE
161 Avenue of the Americas
New York, New York 10013
800-221-2942
www.garrettwade.com
General hand tools and supplies, some power tools

THE HOME DEPOT
2455 Paces Ferry Road
Atlanta, Georgia 30339
800-553-3199 (U.S.)
800-668-2266 (Canada)
www.homedepot.com
Tools, paint, wood, electrical, garden

HOUSE OF TOOLS LTD.
100 Mayfield Common Northwest
Edmonton, Alberta, Canada T5P 4B3
800-661-3987
www.houseoftools.com
Woodworking tools and hardware

JESSEM TOOL COMPANY
171 Robert T. E. # 7 & # 8
Penetanguishene, Ontario,
Canada L9M 1G9
800-436-6799
www.jessem.com
Rout-R-Slide and Rout-R-Lift

JIMMY JIGS
www.jimmyjig.com
Pocket hole jigs

KREG TOOL COMPANY
201 Campus Drive
Huxley, Iowa 50124
800-447-8638
www.kregtool.com
Pocket hole jigs and accessories

LANGEVIN & FOREST
9995 Boulevard Pie IX
Montreal, Quebec, Canada H1Z 3X1
800-889-2060
Tools, wood and books

LEE VALLEY TOOLS LTD.
P.O. Box 1780
Ogdensburg, New York 13669
800-267-8735
www.leevalley.com
Fine woodworking tools and hardware

LOWE'S HOME IMPROVEMENT WAREHOUSE
P.O. Box 1111
North Wilkesboro, North Carolina 28656
800-445-6937
www.lowes.com
Tools, paint, wood, electrical, garden

MCFEELY'S SQUARE DRIVE SCREWS
1620 Wythe Road
P.O. Box 11169
Lynchburg, Virginia 24506-1169
800-443-7937
www.mcfeelys.com
Fasteners

PANOLAM INDUSTRIES INTERNATIONAL, INC.
20 Progress Drive
Shelton, Connecticut 06484
800-672-6652
www.panolam.com
Particleboard supplier

PAXTON WOODCRAFTERS' STORE
4837 Jackson Street
Denver, Colorado 80216
800-332-1331
www.paxton-woodsource.com
Domestic and foreign hardwoods; veneers; books and woodworking tools

PORTER-CABLE
4825 Highway 45 North
P.O. Box 2468
Jackson, Tennessee 38302-2468
800-487-8665
www.porter-cable.com
Woodworking tools

RICHELIEU HARDWARE
7900, West Henri-Bourassa
Ville St-Laurent, Quebec, Canada H4S 1V4
800-619-5446 (U.S.)
800-361-6000 (Canada)
www.richelieu.com
Hardware supplies

ROCKLER WOODWORKING AND HARDWARE
4365 Willow Drive
Medina, Minnesota 55340
800-279-4441
www.rockler.com
Woodworking tools and hardware

S&G SPECIALTY FASTENERS, INC.
2420 Camino Ramon, Suite 320
San Ramon, California 94583
800-743-6916
www.quickscrews.com
Fasteners and drive bits

TOOL TREND LTD.
140 Snow Boulevard
Concord, Ontario, Canada L4K 4C1
416-663-8665
Woodworking tools and hardware

TREND MACHINERY & CUTTING TOOLS LTD.
Odhams Trading Estate
St. Albans Road
Watford, Hertfordshire
WD24 7TR
United Kingdom
0800 487363 (UK)
www.trendmachinery.co.uk
Router cutters and jigs; power tools; woodworking accessories

UNIBOARD CANADA, INC.
3080, Le Carrefour Boulevard, Suite 400
Laval, Quebec, Canada H7T 2R5
800-263-5240
www.uniboard.com
Particleboard and MDF supplier

VAUGHAN
11414 Maple Avenue
Hebron, Illinois 60034
815-648-2446
www.vaughanmfg.com
Hammers and other tools

WOLFCRAFT NORTH AMERICA
1222 West Ardmore Avenue
P.O. Box 687
Itasca, Illinois 60143
630-773-4777
www.wolfcraft.com
Woodworking hardware and accessories

WOODCRAFT
P.O. Box 1686
Parkersburg, West Virginia 26102-1686
800-225-1153
www.woodcraft.com
Woodworking hardware and accessories

WOODWORKER'S HARDWARE
P.O. Box 180
Sauk Rapids, Minnesota 56379-0180
800-383-0130
www.wwhardware.com
Woodworking tools and accessories; finishing supplies; books and plans

WOODWORKER'S SUPPLY
1108 North Glenn Road
Casper, Wyoming 82601
800-645-9292
www.woodworker.com
Woodworking tools and accessories; finishing supplies; books and plans

WORKSHOP SUPPLY
P.O. Box 160
100 Commissioners Street, East
Embro, Ontario, Canada N0J 1J0
800-387-5716
www.workshopsupply.com
Woodworking tools; Jimmy Jigs

index

A
Accessories. *see* Equipment
Applications. *see* Techniques
Arcs, 62

B
Backboard panels, 61

C
Chest of Drawers, 56-67
Child's Wall Clock, 118-123
Clamping the joint, 18
Coffee Tables, 82-89
Collars, 15
Corner joint assembly, 18
Corner miter joints, 20
Countertop backboards, 23
Cutting boards, maintaining grain
    pattern, 94

D
Door construction, 31
Drawer-box construction, 22
Drawer box heights, 65
Drill bits, 15

E
Edge joinery, 19
Edges, installing, 23
End Tables, 82-89
Equipment, 8-15
    collars, 15
    drill bits, 15
    Jimmy Jigs'pocket hole guide sys-
      tem, 11
    Kreg K2000 jig, 10
    Porter-Cable commercial pocket
      hole cutter, 11
    screws, 11
    shop-made jig, 12-14

Trend jig, 10
Exposed pocket holes, 23

F
Face-angle joinery, 20-21
Face-Frame and Case Joinery, 24-33
Framed Mirror, 98-105

H
Hall Table, 90-97
Hardware, 8-15
Hinges, 79

I
Introduction, 6-7

J
Jimmy Jigs'pocket hole guide sys-
    tem, 11

K
Kitchen Display and Storage Cabi-
    net, 68-81
Kreg K2000 jig, 10

L
L-joints, 19
Leg and rail joinery, 22

M
Materials lists
    Chest of Drawers, 59
    Child's Wall Clock, 121
    Coffee Tables, 85
    End Tables, 85
    Face-Frame and Case Joinery, 27
    Framed Mirror, 101
    Hall Table, 93
    Kitchen Display and Storage
      Cabinet, 71

Pendulum Wall Clock, 109
Quilt Rack, 45
Sofa Table, 93
Tall Bookcase, 37
Window Bench, 51

O
Offset joinery, 21

P
Pendulum Wall Clock, 106-117
Plugs, 23, 46, 53, 111
Porter-Cable commercial pocket
    hole cutter, 11
Projects
    Chest of Drawers, 56-67
    Child's Wall Clock, 118-123
    Coffee Tables, 82-89
    End Tables, 82-89
    Face-Frame and Case Joinery, 24-
      33
    Framed Mirror, 98-105
    Hall Table, 90-97
    Kitchen Display and Storage
      Cabinet, 68-81
    Pendulum Wall Clock, 106-117
    Quilt Rack, 42-47
    Sofa Table, 90-97
    Tall Bookcase, 34-41
    Window Bench, 48-55

Q
Quilt Rack, 42-47

S
Screws, 11
Shop-made jig, 12-14
Sofa Table, 90-97
Softwood joinery, 18
Suppliers, 124-125

T
T-joints, 19
Tall Bookcase, 34-41
Techniques, 16-23
    clamping the joint, 18
    corner joint assembly, 18
    corner miter joints, 20
    countertop backboards, 23
    drawer-box construction, 22
    edge joinery, 19
    edges, installing, 23
    exposed pocket holes, 23
    face-angle joinery, 20-21
    L-joints, 19
    leg and rail joinery, 22
    offset joinery, 21
    softwood joinery, 18
    T-joints, 19
    testing the joint, 18
Testing the joint, 18
Trend jig, 10

V
Veneer, trimming, 38

W
Window Bench, 48-55

The Best Woodworking Projects come from Popular Woodworking Books!

The ultimate one-stop resource for woodworkers! This guide gives you instant access to real solutions and solid advice for every woodworking dilemma. You'll find a variety of key topics including wood, hardware, shop math, routers, hand tools, measuring, power tools, adhesives, sharpening, finishing and much more.

ISBN 1-55870-632-1, paperback, 144 pages, #70579-K

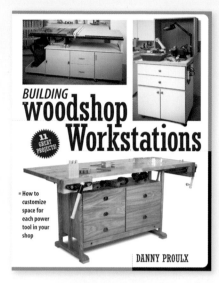

Build the workshop of your dreams! Danny Proulx provides detailed plans and easy-to-follow instructions for building 12 completely self-contained units for every tool and related accessory. Each design ensures that the wrenches, blades, jigs and attachments for all of your tools are within arm's reach.

ISBN 1-55870-637-2, paperback, 128 pages, #70585-K

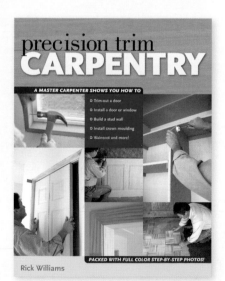

Here's all the instruction you need to craft professional-level precision trim carpentry. Start-to-finish guidelines and step-by-step photos that make any project easy. Want to trim a door? Replace a window? Install wainscot panels? Whatever the job at hand, master carpenter Rick Williams makes sure you have the information you need to do it right.

ISBN 1-55870-636-4, paperback, 128 pages, #70584-K

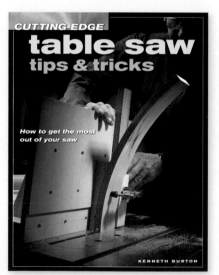

Ken Burton illustrates just how important and efficient your table saw can be with dozens of tricks, techniques and jigs that cover the entire range of what a table saw can do, everything from crafting precision joinery to accurately cutting pieces to size. Each technique is easy-to-do, safe to execute, and certain to save you time and money.

ISBN 1-55870-623-2, paperback, 128 pages, #70569-K

These books and other fine Popular Woodworking titles are available from your local bookstore, online supplier or by calling 1-800-448-0915.